Jacqueline Escoïme

REBUILD YOUR HEALTH, RECLAIM YOUR LIFE

*A Guide to Healing Yourself Naturally
and Creating Lifelong Wellness*

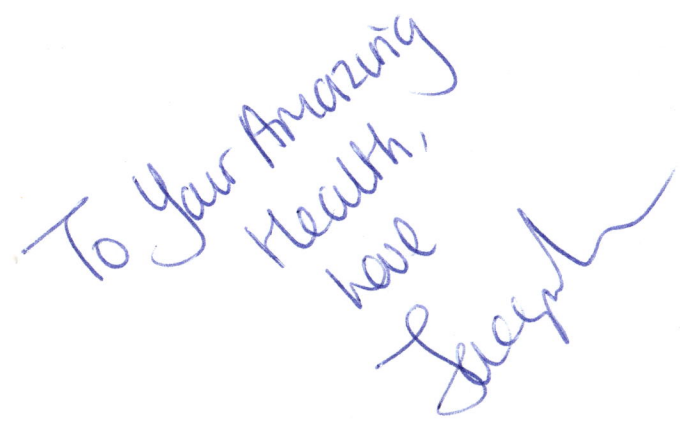

AUSTIN MACAULEY PUBLISHERS™
LONDON · CAMBRIDGE · NEW YORK · SHARJAH

A CIP catalogue record for this title is available from the British Library.

ISBN 9781528911719 (Paperback)
ISBN 9781528959889 (ePub e-book)

www.austinmacauley.com

First published by the author (2016)

This revised edition published (2019)
Austin Macauley Publishers Ltd
25 Canada Square
Canary Wharf
London
E14 5LQ

*To those who believe better is possible
and dare to think differently*

Acknowledgements

To all those on my journey who opened my eyes to healing and health,
thank you.

To every practitioner I initially thought a little crazy, I love and thank you.

To the women who came before, on whose shoulders I stand
and who taught me well, I love and thank you.

To my children who gave me a reason to live, I am eternally grateful.
You are my joy.

To Lynne and Karen, the sisters who believed in this book and in me,
I am blessed to call you my friends. Thank you.

Contents

About the Author 7

A Note from Jacqueline 8

Introduction 9

SECTION 1: START WHERE YOU ARE WITH WHAT YOU HAVE 11

    My Journey 15

    The Letter I Wrote to My Children 18

    Begin Your Rebuild 20

SECTION 2: THE STORY OF YOU 25

    Worksheet 27

    Top to Toe Review 56

    Understanding Your Symptoms 62

    Putting It All Together 73

SECTION 3: YOUR FUEL ASSESSMENT 81

    What Do You Want More Of? 88

    What About Water? 96

    Add and Avoid: A Simple Long-Term Plan 103

    Cravings, Stress Eating and Dieting 118

    Step Away from the Sugar 121

    How to Re-Programme Your Palate 123

    Food Trends 126

    Encountering Resistance! 128

SECTION 4: SETTING UP YOUR SUPPORT 131

    7 Steps to Solid Support 134

SECTION 5: MY 3 GOLDEN RULES OF REBUILDING **141**

    Rule Number 1 – Release 143

    Types of Techniques 148

    Rule Number 2 – Real Rest and Relaxation 159

    Taking Time Out 163

    Rule Number 3 – Remember. 171

SECTION 6: CREATING THE NEW YOU **177**

    Seeing Yourself Differently: A Whole Body Exercise 180

    Releasing Trapped Emotions 185

    A Message to You from Your Body 186

SECTION 7: MINDING YOUR HEALTH **188**

    A Few Words on Cancer 194

    Changing Your Perception About What's Possible 196

    Losing Your Labels 199

    Vision Your Health 205

SECTION 8: THE 7 BIGGEST BLOCKS TO GREAT HEALTH **216**

    Block No 1 – Fear 218

    Block No 2 – Lack 227

    Block No 3 – The Ego 232

    Block No 4 – Forgiveness 235

    Block No 5 – Gratitude 237

    Block No 6 – Taking Action 240

    Block No 7 – Support 243

    Getting to the Gift 245

SECTION 9: YOUR 8-STEP ONGOING PROGRAMME **252**

SECTION 10: RESOURCES **256**

About the Author

Writer and mother Jacqueline Escolme battled serious illness from her mid-twenties and spent ten years studying alternative health and the mind-body connection after being written off by her doctor. This life-changing journey into self-help and personal development revolutionised her approach to wellness and gave her a unique understanding of the human body.

While living as an expatriate in Russia, America and South Africa, Jacqueline studied and explored everything from "old-fashioned" to "unconventional" health practices. She qualified as a Natural Nutritionist and Transformational Coach and continually tested and applied her learning to develop the unique and truly integrated mind-body process she describes in *Rebuild Your Health, Reclaim Your Life*.

Jacqueline now resides in the UK, living a life she once thought impossible, enjoying vibrant health and vitality. She remains an eternal student, passionate about health and supporting others to achieve true healing and well-being, faster.

A Note from Jacqueline

This book contains advice and information relating to health care. I am legally required to state that it is not intended to replace medical advice and should be used to supplement regular care by your doctor, although of course, ultimately you, and only you, are responsible TO your body and FOR your health.

Your results will vary according to the effort you put into your rebuild. While all efforts have been made to assure the accuracy of the information contained in this book, at the date of publication, as the author, I am legally advised to disclaim any responsibility for medical outcomes that may occur as a result of applying the methods outlined in this book – even though they worked for me and many others.

Introduction

The aim of this book is to demystify the process of being and feeling well, written by someone who's had to learn the hard way!

First, let me say this is NOT a diet book or a new fad. There are nutritional guidelines to help you, but this is primarily a book about understanding how you got to a point of illness and how to create health and vitality instead.

If you are caught up in an illness, allergy or any kind of condition that affects your health and wellbeing, then I'd like to show you how you can create achievable change and long lasting health. This approach is not a sugarcoated pill that will magic away your symptoms. It's an "I've been there, I've done it and here's what worked for me."

Take a moment and ask yourself: what if, instead of your illness having all the power, you did?

What if you knew how to create health instead of toxicity? How would your life look then?

Would you love to know how to let your natural and inherent good health re-emerge, just by creating the right conditions?

Would you LOVE some simply put, easy to follow information to get you heading back towards health, and the life you want?

Yes?

Then it's no accident you're reading this book.

This is a revolutionary way to think about and create health. You can get the best out of your body and your life and you can start right now, at whatever stage of health or illness you're at.

If you find yourself questioning why you are unwell, from generalised fatigue to full-blown disease, rest assured, you are not alone. Many people are looking for a simpler way. My hope is that this book, in some part, illuminates it.

If you picked up this book, the chances are you need it. Maybe you're suffering with illness. Perhaps you experience a persistent low-grade fatigue you can't shift. You may feel lethargic, despondent or never fully happy or able to experience joy. You may have symptoms, allergies and intolerances that you've coped with for so long they've become a part of you and you can't remember how life ever was before they arrived.

Are you ready to be free of them?

My advice is this – Start right now, wherever you are, with whatever you bring to the table and begin your rebuild. It will not all be plain sailing. I can tell you from experience that there will be highs and lows, but I encourage you to hold your course, apply this process and keep moving in the direction of health. The knowledge I gained from over ten years of rebuilding myself has been poured into these page with love, in the hope that it will empower you and enable you to achieve results much faster.

I am an average woman who chose to see health differently and if I can do it, you can too.

SECTION 1

START WHERE YOU ARE WITH WHAT YOU HAVE

These days it's relatively rare to meet someone who doesn't have a health issue. From allergies to asthma and full-blown disease, ill health seems to be everywhere and many people are in a state of overwhelm, bombarded by contradicting information.

Are you someone who's so used to having symptoms that the medication you started taking as a coping strategy has become a way of life?

I know how it feels to be dependent on tablets. To wait, as though life is on hold, for blood test results, or the next scan. Illness can exert so much control over your life that, in addition to your symptoms, it becomes draining emotionally, financially and energetically.

Whether you're experiencing the first niggling symptoms of illness or you're looking back at your life wondering how things got to this point. Now is the time to get interested in your illness and yourself. The truth is that no matter which doctors you've seen or what medication you're taking, the only person who can ultimately heal you, is YOU.

Medication may certainly remove your symptoms, for as long as you continue to take it, but to truly heal means to not need the medication, because your symptoms no longer exist. To me, that is health.

In this book, I'm going to show you how to create conditions for health, using a simple law of cause and effect. In essence, if you address the cause, you get a better effect, which is vibrant, energised health. The sad fact is most people don't realise they are consciously and unconsciously creating conditions for anything but health.

Who am I to say all this? Some fancy doctor?

Nope, just an average woman who became severely ill, tried conventional medicine without success, then spent 10 years studying alternative forms of medicine, healing, nutrition and psychology and applying this learning to rebuild myself and my life.

While I'm trained in many health disciplines and, as part of my journey, qualified as a Natural Nutritionist, I am not a medical doctor – and that is exactly my point.

If, as an average woman, I can rebuild myself then so can you.

The reason I wrote this book is that you may not want to spend ten years studying. You may not feel well enough, or be able to commit to the financial investment, that dedication to learning requires. By sharing what I've learnt and tested, I hope you won't need, or have to. Yes, you may feel drawn to learn more as you begin to feel better, and I would highly encourage that, but in the meantime, I wrote this book to help you rebuild yourself faster using my knowledge and experience.

If you're ready to create change in your health. I'll show you where to start and what to do, and I'll keep it simple. No overloading you with anatomy and physiology. Just easy to apply information and support tools you can use to empower yourself to recovery. Fast.

Wondering if this is for you?

Do you hear yourself think or say any of the following:

I'm not myself.

I'm always tired.

My… (insert body part) …hurts.

I don't have the energy.

I've got a… (insert symptom).

Why won't this… (insert symptom)… go away?

Why do I feel like this?

Why is this happening to me?

I feel anxious about this symptom.

I'm… any label.

Yes? Read on!

Are you frustrated with the answers you've been given? Do you find conventional solutions unhelpful? Are you tired of relying on medication and ready to get on with the rest of your life?

In every case, I hear you. ☺

I wrote this book because 14 years ago I was in the same position, and I was terrified.

My Journey

These days my early twenties feel like a blur.

I worked hard and played hard, in what was pretty much a subconscious effort to numb emotional trauma from my childhood. I didn't realise at the time, but I was constantly trying to prove my self-worth. If I was earning good money and regularly being promoted, that was a sign I was worthy. If I had lots of friends, boyfriends and wild parties to go to, that was another. Keeping all this up meant I was in overdrive all the time. Relentlessly pushing myself to achieve something, anything, to make myself feel worthy and lovable.

One day, I woke feeling unusually sluggish. I tried to push through, but this time I couldn't ignore my body. Particularly, as my legs would no longer support me! It was bizarre and frightening. I remember crawling across the floor to call for help as the world around me started spinning. A trip to hospital proved inconclusive, so I was sent home to rest and it was passed off as a strange virus.

I thought it was a blip. It was actually "Welcome to your new life".

Where once I'd had energy, now I had exhaustion and dizziness. I lost 14lbs in two weeks without trying. I could barely concentrate and felt like I was passing out all the time. I went to my doctor who told me I had "Post-viral syndrome" which he didn't really know how to explain. It was months later, through much persistence, that I managed to see a specialist who tested my thyroid and told me I had 50% extra thyroxin (a thyroid hormone) in my body. In other words, I was severely hyperthyroid.

In a matter of fact way, I was told I would be on drugs for the rest of my life and would probably have my thyroid cut out at some point. This wasn't exactly how I'd imagined my twenty-fifth year of life!

Reluctantly, I took the drugs, but despite being on medication, I quickly developed a host of new and confusing symptoms that didn't fit the typical "overactive" thyroid picture. I followed my doctor's advice and tried to manage my symptoms with medication but fast-forward six years, two countries, another job and two children later and I was a wreck.

I still had thyroid issues but now the rest of my body had joined in! I suffered from chronic fatigue, adrenal exhaustion, endocrine malfunction, allergies and intolerances, severe hypoglycaemia, panic attacks, lowgrade depression and persistent anaemia.

I felt as though my body had gone haywire! I was constantly exhausted with brain fog, dizziness and nausea. Most frightening of all, I felt perpetually off-balance and about to pass out. I had blood tests, brain scans and x-rays but my symptoms were so diverse my doctor didn't seem to be able to give me a diagnosis, or a prescription.

By 2001, my routine looked something like this:

> 9pm collapse into bed exhausted.
>
> 12am and 5am – breastfeed my baby son.
>
> 6am – get up with the baby and my 3-year-old daughter, feed them and get them ready for the day.
>
> 8am – retire to a horizontal position on the floor, unable to function, wondering how I was going to get through the rest of the day.

At the time, my husband typically worked a fourteen-hour day and so wasn't around much to help. My family were on another continent and the few friends I had were mums with small kids of their own so my immediate support was ZERO.

My symptoms ruled my life. Some days, I was too terrified to drive in case I passed out and caused an accident, injuring my children or anyone else. I can vividly remember being terrified to bathe my baby son in case I passed out and he drowned.

I could no longer walk more than 100m without needing to sit, or preferably, lie down and my digestive system could cope with fewer and fewer foods. I felt isolated, desperately fighting the realisation that my body was giving up on me.

It was terrifying and frustrating. I had always seen myself as physically strong. I was used to pushing myself on every level and achieving, but now it seemed my body had nothing left to give.

When my symptoms got really bad, I started admitting myself to the emergency room at the hospital and begging them to help. They'd let me lie on a bed for a while, do a brief check and then tell me I wasn't an emergency and to go and see my doctor.

Eventually, even my doctor admitted that due to the diversity of my symptoms, she didn't know how to treat me, or perhaps where to start. She gave up and offered me Prozac as a last resort.

Something in me clicked. I knew that Prozac wasn't the answer. I left her office, knowing I would never see her again. I have never felt so alone or so sure I was going to die. It was without question, the low point of my life.[*]

What made it even harder was my shame at what was happening to my body. I felt like such a failure that I did not share the details of my illness with anyone. I put on a brave face to those that saw me, and my family and friends who knew me well enough to see behind the mask, were too far away to be able to notice. Even my husband did not realise the full extent of my condition. Our lives seemed to be pulling us in different directions and his usual response to my health complaint was "It's all in your head".

My life as I knew it seemed to be over. I felt cheated. I was furious, and very, very afraid. Dying seemed inevitable but, as parents the world over will understand, the thought of leaving my baby and toddler to grow up without a mother was more than I could bear. It took a while, and it broke my heart, but I sat and wrote a letter to my children. I hoped someone would read it to them after I was gone as they were far too young to remember me in person.

A copy of the letter is on the next page – before you read it, let me warn you it's emotional. If it's distressing for you then feel free to return to it later.

---

[*] I know any doctor reading this will say, 'She wasn't about to die,' and after years of study, I'd probably agree with them, but let me tell you, when your body gives up on you repeatedly, in the absence of another solution you consider what seems inevitable.

The Letter I Wrote to My Children

To my darling children,

I'm writing this in case something happens to me and I don't get the chance to see you grow up into gorgeous, beautiful people. I want you to know that I love you both more than words can ever express and you mean the world to me.

If anything ever happens to me, never feel alone. Know that I will be watching over you and guiding you always.

I want you to look after each other, always, and especially look after Daddy. Always follow your hearts and your dreams and never give them up. We are all here for a purpose – try to find yours and fulfil it. In doing so, you will make yourselves happy.

Never be afraid of love – embrace it and relish it for it is the key to everything. Cherish your friends and your family, they are precious and will always love and support you.

Have fun and remember to laugh every day – it's good for you. Surround yourselves with people and things that make you happy and remember the path to material wealth doesn't always lead to happiness. The path to fulfilment isn't always easy either but never give up on your dream – anything is possible!

Live life to the full. Nourish yourselves and nurture your bodies, they have to get you through life. Most of all, nourish your souls, they have to get you through eternity!

Enjoy yourselves, my beautiful children. I will always love and adore you and you will always be surrounded by that. Know that I am with you always, loving and protecting.

All my eternal love,

Mama xxxxx

The reason I included this letter is to emphasise that wherever you're at in your health story, believe me when I say, I can understand and empathise. Whether you're tired and stressed or feeling you're at death's door, I can relate. That's why I wrote this book.

Here's what you need to know – I firmly believe that you always have a choice.

You CAN create health. It is POSSIBLE.

In an unexpected way, writing the letter to my kids became a catalyst for me. It was a point of surrender. It was the moment I gave up fighting my body and starting listening to it instead.

Gradually, from that low of heartbreak and despair, I rebuilt my body and my life. There was no miracle cure, although I certainly prayed for one on many occasions. Instead, through persistence, education and working through the information I share with you in this book, I experienced many small miracles, which when put together, led to the reinstatement of my health. In following this example of what's possible and using the information I share, my hope is that you will be able to do the same.

You may well experience instant benefits from this book. I believe a mental shift can facilitate an immediate physical shift. However, please understand it is your sustained effort and practice that will create lasting wellness and happiness.

As you begin now, trust that your body knows what to do. If you create the conditions for health, it can and will follow through.

Begin Your Rebuild

I'm not sure if this is for me. I think I'm pretty healthy, but I still don't feel great.

Isn't it frustrating when you're doing what you think is right, or what you've been told to do, but not getting the results you want?

The truth is that most of us have layers upon layers of toxicity that exercising regularly, eating salad and getting seven to eight hours sleep, are NEVER going to shift.

Add to this the truckload of emotional baggage we accumulate and you have the perfect recipe for illness.

The world we live in today is more polluted and toxic than ever and our stress levels are soaring. You think you're healthy? If you're tired, emotional or suffering from symptoms, then you're not well, and you know this, or you wouldn't be reading this book.

How does it work?

First, I'm going to show you how to get back in touch with your body. Sound a little crazy? It's not. If the oil light comes on in your car, you do something about it. Do you do this when something's not right in your body?

Most of us take for granted that our bodies ferry us around, heal when we cut ourselves and oxygenate us through breathing. Yet apart from feeding, washing, clothing ourselves and maybe a bit of exercise, we often don't think about supporting it much beyond that. I certainly didn't.

Your body is the most advanced piece of kit on the planet and the better you maintain it, the better it performs. The problem is that most of us seem to have lost the maintenance manual! In all honesty, we were never taught this stuff. We've been operating from old beliefs that simply don't work.

Now is your chance to change that. I want to re-frame the way you think about and nourish your body, and in doing so, change your health for the better. I'm going to give you the tools to rebuild yourself so you can move from feeling weak and sick, to strong, empowered and fully able to support yourself and your loved ones in vibrant, fabulous health.

Is it complicated?

If you're not coping well right now, don't worry. I appreciate you may not be at full strength, so this book is divided into sections to make it easy to read, learn from and put into practice.

You'll have the opportunity to play detective in your own life and what you reveal will guide you to understanding how you got to this point. Be honest but compassionate with yourself. It is only by exploring your own case that you will gain insights and unravel the ill health you are experiencing.

Resist the temptation to be afraid or overwhelmed. This process will not drain you but make you stronger. Some exercises may appear simple but try not to rush through them. Take time to answer honestly – and don't be surprised if information drops in some time later, when you least expect it.

I encourage you to keep your responses to yourself for now and avoid the temptation to discuss potentially painful episodes or events. You do not need to re-live how you got to this point, merely to order it, so you can assess and begin to understand what's happened to your vitality and your health.

This book is a tool for you to use. Write in it. Fill in the worksheets and keep it just for you. Getting all your information in one place will be very useful as you go through the process of rebuilding, so don't leave anything out.

How long will this take?

There is no right and wrong time frame when it comes to your rebuild, there is only YOUR time frame. Work at a speed that feels right and be consistent and committed. Do it daily and your life will change.

Where do I start?

Right here. Right now.

Sometimes we tell ourselves we need to change before we start a new programme. It's the "I'll do that once I've done this" thinking.

Call it what you like, it's denial, procrastination or self-sabotage. Recognise it for what it is and you'll take the power out of it. Read on and I'll give you the tools to kick it into touch every time it raises its head. If you want to be well, there's no better starting place than the present. You don't need anything other than yourself. No special equipment or PhD in biology. Just you.

Remember this is a process. It works best if you engage in it from beginning to end and follow the chapters sequentially. It's specifically designed to be of maximum benefit to you in this way, so avoid jumping ahead as you may miss vital information.

The worksheets in the book are for you to complete and add to, as information drops in. In my experience, this can be anything from hours to days or weeks later! These worksheets are a valuable source of info for you to refer back to and check your progress against. Fill them out. Use them.

At the end of each section, you will find journal space. Use this to note down the thoughts, ideas and challenges that came up for you. You can work on or refer back to them as you move through your rebuild. It can be as simple as noting down feelings and emotions, areas where you felt resistance, exercises you found useful, or things you'd like to share on the Rebuild Your Health Facebook page. Go to **www.rebuildyourhealthreclaimyourlife.com** and click on the Facebook icon.

Finally, the Resources section at the end provides you with more information that I hope will serve and support you in regaining your health.

Take a deep breath and release any stress you're feeling. In section 2, you'll begin the journey of understanding how you got to this point.

Journal Space

SECTION 2

THE STORY OF YOU

Most of us think we know ourselves but I'd like to take you on a journey to learn about your health issues in a much broader way. Instead of thinking about a symptom or problem in isolation, we're going to relate it to the rest of your life, including your family, your work and all stress therein. By making connections in this way you will begin to see that illness is a process of progression towards disease or imbalance, just as health is a progression towards wellness and balance.

If you think you know yourself well, be prepared, this can be an eye-opener! As you dive into the worksheet, try to imagine that you're doing a giant jigsaw puzzle, and the picture you're creating is YOU. You're going to piece together all the clues in your life that have brought you to this point of health, whatever that may look like.

Set aside all blame, shame and judgement that may try to creep in. It has no place here. Here, we simply honour the story of you. Remember, be honest as you complete the following worksheet, or as honest as you can remember! This is just for you.

Worksheet

The Story of You

What's your biggest health issue right now?

How does it show up as one or more physical symptoms?

Where are they located in your body?

How do you feel emotionally?

Where do your emotional symptoms feel like they reside in your physical body? If you are unsure, close your eyes and bring the emotional issue to your mind. Now place your hand on the part of your body that feels the discomfort from the emotion most strongly. Without feeling the need to judge, just note where the discomfort is felt.

I feel discomfort…

Your Family

Think about the people in your family. Focus on your blood relatives and the illnesses or symptoms that are currently, or have been part of their lives. Note them down against each person, if applicable.

Grandparents:

Parents:

Siblings:

If your loved ones have passed on, is there another relative or family friend who can help you with symptoms, diseases or cause of death.

If you are adopted and do not have access to information about your health heritage, do not worry. This is an aid in your detective work not a prerequisite for a successful Rebuild.

Starting at the beginning

It's time to look at your life and we're going right back to your childhood. If you have parents, or older generations of your family who can help you with information, great. If not, your memories will still work perfectly and you'll be amazed at what you do remember, even if it takes a few days!

A word of caution here. If you have trauma in your past and you hold a particular person, people or event responsible, do not get caught up in this. It's a piece of your jigsaw puzzle that you are simply using for information. Understand that if you choose to feel blame against someone else this creates negativity in you and ultimately decreases the energy you have available for rebuilding your health.

Note down the event and the effect on your health, take a deep breath, let it go and move on to the next question.

Your childhood

Many of us are still carrying around things we internalised as children and these show up in the body as unresolved stress, which is another name for illness. A parent's divorce, moving schools, being bullied or persistent bouts of tonsillitis or illness are all experiences that belong in this section.

If you are lucky enough to have parents or other relatives around who can help you, great. If not, or if you can't remember, don't worry. This is not a test! Whatever comes up for you will be perfect for right now.

As you work through, try and put approximate ages against anything you have written as this will help fit the other jigsaw pieces together later.

Do you remember any significant incidents or events from your childhood?

Were there any situations or circumstances that you remember as painful or traumatic?

What effect did they have on you?

Do you remember any physical trauma or illness?

If you don't consciously remember things, have you heard your parents or family members talk about stories that involved you?

Note down any memories that seem important.

It's very common for kids to have accidents as they grow and explore but were there any broken bones or serious accidents that you remember?

Do you remember any recurring symptoms or health issues?

Were you medicated for anything on a regular basis?

Teenage Years

Adolescence is a very important time for all of us. Our bodies have the huge job of turning us from children into adults. It's one of the great transitions of our lives and this is often when symptoms show up.

For Women:

What age did your periods start?

Were they painful?

If you had a child in your teenage years, were there any problems with the pregnancy or birth?

Note down all miscarriages and abortions too, these are traumatic events.

For Everyone:

Do you recall having any illnesses or symptoms during puberty? (Generally between the ages of 12–16 years).

Were there any major events or traumas?

Did you take any medication on a regular basis?

Was there a time during puberty when you drank heavily, smoked or took recreational drugs?

Did you experience any health effects or symptoms as a result?

Is there a symptom or condition you had as a child that got worse or better during your teenage years?

The Decades of Your Life

Now it's time to explore each decade of your life from the perspective of your health and its improvement or deterioration. Make notes under each heading, paying particular attention to emotional highs and lows and any persistent, recurring or unusual symptoms.

Also, add any stress you may have suffered and remember to put an approximate age against each entry if you can (I know for some of us it's been a while!)

Some decades may be full and some relatively empty. This is perfectly normal.

Twenties

What emotional highs do you remember? For example, marriage, childbirth, career achievements, travel experiences, relationships…

What emotional lows did you experience? For example bereavement, grief, divorce, relationship issues, house move…

Were there any accidents, surgery, childbirth, miscarriages?

Any other issues, symptoms or significant change in your life at this time?

How they were treated?

Use of cigarettes, alcohol, drugs?

Did you take medication on a regular basis?

How was your sense of purpose? General level of happiness and health?

Thirties

What emotional highs do you remember? For example, marriage, childbirth, career achievements, travel experiences, relationships…

What emotional lows did you experience? For example bereavement, grief, divorce, relationship issues, house move…

Were there any accidents, surgery, childbirth, miscarriages?

Any other issues, symptoms or significant change in your life at this time?

How they were treated?

Use of cigarettes, alcohol, drugs?

Did you take medication on a regular basis?

How was your sense of purpose? General level of happiness and health?

Forties

What emotional highs do you remember? For example, marriage, childbirth, career achievements, travel experiences, relationships…

What emotional lows did you experience? For example bereavement, grief, divorce, relationship issues, house move…

Were there any accidents, surgery, childbirth, miscarriages?

Any other issues, symptoms or significant change in your life at this time?

How they were treated?

Use of cigarettes, alcohol, drugs?

Did you take medication on a regular basis?

How was your sense of purpose? General level of happiness and health?

Fifties

What emotional highs do you remember? For example, marriage, career achievements, travel experiences, relationships…

What emotional lows did you experience? For example bereavement, grief, divorce, relationship issues, house move…

Were there any accidents, surgery?

Any other issues, symptoms or significant change in your life at this time?

How they were treated?

Use of cigarettes, alcohol, drugs?

Did you take medication on a regular basis?

How was your sense of purpose? General level of happiness and health?

Sixties

What emotional highs do you remember? For example, marriage, career achievements, travel experiences, relationships…

What emotional lows did you experience? For example bereavement, grief, divorce, relationship issues, house move…

Were there any accidents, surgery?

Any other issues, symptoms or significant change in your life at this time?

How they were treated?

Use of cigarettes, alcohol, drugs?

Did you take medication on a regular basis?

How was your sense of purpose? General level of happiness and health?

Seventies

What emotional highs do you remember? For example, marriage, career achievements, travel experiences, relationships…

What emotional lows did you experience? For example bereavement, grief, divorce, relationship issues, house move…

Were there any accidents, surgery?

Any other issues, symptoms or significant change in your life at this time?

How they were treated?

Use of cigarettes, alcohol, drugs?

Did you take medication on a regular basis?

How was your sense of purpose? General level of happiness and health?

Eighties

What emotional highs do you remember?

What emotional lows did you experience? For example bereavement, grief, divorce, relationship issues, house move…

Were there any accidents, surgery?

Any other issues, symptoms or significant change in your life at this time?

How they were treated?

Use of cigarettes, alcohol, drugs?

Did you take medication on a regular basis?

How was your sense of purpose? General level of happiness and health?

Nineties

What emotional highs do you remember?

What emotional lows did you experience? For example bereavement, grief, divorce, relationship issues, house move…

Were there any accidents, surgery?

Any other issues, symptoms or significant change in your life at this time?

How they were treated?

Use of cigarettes, alcohol, drugs?

Did you take medication on a regular basis?

How was your sense of purpose? General level of happiness and health?

If you are over one hundred, please feel free to continue. It's an interesting exercise for anyone to do but by reaching the milestone of a century, I suspect you have looked after yourself well and probably have an exceptional genetic ancestry, so well done to you!

Here's to your continued longevity. ☺

What if I can't remember certain dates or conditions?

Don't worry and don't try and force it. Over the next few days, you are likely to find that dates, incidents and events will drop into your consciousness quite out of the blue. Keep a pen and paper handy so that you can jot them down and then add them to the worksheet.

Wow, I didn't realise I'd been through so much.

Until it's all laid out in front of us, it's easy to forget how much we've been through. ☺

Resist the temptation to dive into any pain this brings up for you. Investing energy into the past only limits what you have available for your rebuild and your future.

Take a moment and re-frame everything that's happened to this point as a necessary part of your journey. This is how you got here. This is where you are and who you are. This is the beginning of your rebuild. Only you get to choose what your potential for health is.

Why is the health of my family members important?

While you are very much a human being in your own right, you had to come from somewhere and that means you are, in part, a product of those who came before you.

Looking back at your ancestry gives you an opportunity to identify any patterns of illness or similar diseases. We're checking what's in your closet so to speak, but in case you have a lot of disease in your family and you're now panicking, let me be very clear. I am not someone who believes that disease is automatically handed down from one generation to the next. According to my years of study, a genetic disorder MAY or MAY NOT be inherited.

The most pertinent argument I can find is this:

> *'If I have a history of, for example, heart disease in my family, it may mean that if I consistently create conditions for toxicity in my body, my cells MAY know how to produce heart disease more easily than another illness. It is not a foregone conclusion that this will be the case.'*

So if you have a lot of cancer in your family, it MAY pre-dispose you towards cancer, rather than say, a stroke, but it depends on the condition of your health. What science proves repeatedly is that we are all individuals and so are our patterns of disease, so don't get too hung up on your family history right now and don't close the book now and assume the inevitable. It's not the case and it does not mean that great health is out of the question for you.

A well-nourished, cleansed and supported body will determine its own fate and you are very much behind the wheel. ☺

How to Use "The Story of You" Worksheet

Start with a quick assessment of your ancestry. Look for common conditions or complaints. There may not be anything, or you may see a history of similar symptoms.

Now compare this information to the conditions or symptoms of your life to date. Have you experienced similar symptoms or something totally different?

Remember this information is for your learning only. Do not get caught up in the drama around any diseases. If your health seems to be moving in a particular direction or towards a named condition then this is just a helpful snapshot of where you are now.

Awareness is essential to healing. It's the first step towards health. Look at your symptoms through the decades. Notice which have worsened or improved and see if they tie in with anything else that was going on in your life around that time. In particular, look at your teenage years and see if illness cropped up there and then reared its head again later in life.

Pay particular attention to acute episodes.

What's an Acute Illness/Episode?

Acutes are illnesses or symptoms that flare up quickly and then dissipate just as quickly when the body's immune system kicks in and dispatches them! In other words, acutes are the body's way of trying to burn off toxicity. A fever that knocked you out for a couple of days is a good example.

As you study your health history pay particular attention to where your health issues change from being more acute and sudden onset (e.g. tonsillitis) to longer term, chronic conditions (e.g. allergies, eczema). This may happen over a period of years or decades and it gives you an idea of your toxicity levels.

Notice if acute symptoms disappear at a certain age but then other symptoms materialise and become chronic.

What's a Chronic Illness?

A chronic condition is a long-term illness that you just can't seem to get rid of. When the condition becomes chronic, it usually means the body is lacking the vital energy required to produce an acute, resulting in a perpetual low-grade symptom.

It might be fatigue you can't shake off, a cough that never leaves you or a persistent irritation like eczema. Chronics often require regular medication e.g. antihistamines for allergies, or a lifestyle change like avoiding gluten if you've become coeliac.

Look at your worksheet and see if there was a point when your symptoms shifted from more acute to more chronic. Can you get an idea of how long your body has been in a chronic state?

A Word About Toxicity

If you are someone who has regular spates of acute symptoms, try to identify a pattern.

Are they seasonal?

Annual?

In direct correlation with work or emotional stress?

Look for trigger points in your history to help you make sense of this.

All of this should give you an indication of your toxicity levels over time and how your body is handling illness.

Again, please bear in mind, everyone's health story is different. There is no right or wrong answer. This information is just for you and now it's time to build on it further to give you more answers.

Top to Toe Review

You've been through a historical review of your health and now it's time to evaluate where you are today, right here right now!

Answer the following questions, noting down any symptoms you have. This may jolt your memory back to a time when you experienced something similar. If so, go back and note it down in the previous worksheet, under the appropriate age range. This will help provide the most detailed picture of your health.

Rate your current energy levels from 1 to 10, with 10 being the highest. For example, if you wake before your alarm, leap out of bed and feel fully energised all day then this would be a 10.

Energy level =

In the same way, rate your ability to concentrate with 10 being the highest and 1 being the lowest.

Concentration =

How about your memory? Can you remember things from two years ago/ a long time ago?

Long term memory =

How about short term memory? Do the names of people you saw yesterday suddenly drop out of your head during conversation?

Short term memory =

Don't be dissuaded if your ratings are low. That's why you're reading this book! My energy levels went from a 2 to a 10 and when you look back on these answers in 6 or 12 months, I hope you'll experience a similar trend.

Now it's time to go over your body and note down anything you experience or are unhappy with. In each case, make honest notes right next to each title, no matter how crazy or unrelated they seem. If it's relevant to you, or the way you feel about a part of your body, write it down. ☺

Hair – Greasy? Thinning?

Skin – Dryness? Eczema? Rashes or irritation?

Head – Headaches or migraines?

Nose – Allergic sneezing, rhinitis or sinus problems?

Throat – Sore throats or tonsillitis?

Ears – Blocked or ringing? Frequent ear infections?

Chest and lungs – Sighing? Shortness of breath? Wheezing? Asthma? Pneumonia?

Stomach and digestion – Bloating? Gas? Flatulence? Nausea or vomiting? Food poisoning? Generally tired and sluggish after eating?

Bowels – I know this is an area some people are uncomfortable thinking about but bear with me. Recognise that your body is built to release toxicity through the bowels and if this fundamental part of the cleansing process gets blocked then it quickly gives rise to other symptoms.

Have you ever experienced repeated constipation or diarrhoea?

Do you have a bowel movement every day?

Morning or evening or both?

Are your stools firm and brown?

Urination – Any pain or problem passing urine? Colour?

Legs, knees, ankles – Any problems or aches and pains in these areas?

Feet – Warts, fungal infections, toenail problems?

Now mentally scan your body one last time. Are there any general aches and pains you'd like to make a note of? If something else is niggling you then write it here.

Other notes:

Wow. That's you, in a nutshell. Past and present both on worksheets. Great information for you to use to create a healthier future.

Take a deep breath and consider everything you've revealed to yourself. How do you feel about it?

Make a note of emotions that come up. Name them if you can and briefly close your eyes, concentrate on each emotion and try to identify where in your body they seem to be stored.

Emotions I'm feeling right now and where I'm feeling them:

Reflect back on the first question in "The Story of You" worksheet at the beginning of section two. Do you still agree with what you wrote as your most pressing health issue?

If something else is coming up, write it below and don't be surprised if it's emotional rather than physical, for example, "I don't feel loved" instead of "I feel tired all the time".

My most pressing health issue is:

All this information will be useful later in the book so write down anything that this exercise has stirred up for you.

Now take a few deep breaths and consciously release. This is part of your journey. See all this information as a blessing on your rebuild, not as the millstone that is lodged around your neck.

This information will empower you into health if you let it.

OMG, I've got so many symptoms. I should call my doctor!

Okay, let's keep things in perspective. Yes, you have just completed a thorough head to toe assessment and thought about every symptom you have, rather than the isolated ones you may be receiving treatment for. This is unlikely to change the way your doctor will prescribe medication to you. Read on to find out why.

Understanding Your Symptoms

Modern, or conventional medicine treats your illness according to your symptoms. The job of your doctor is to recognise and treat the symptoms you present him/her with. Doctors typically treat a snapshot of where you are at a particular moment and they're trained to give you medication to alleviate your symptoms.

My approach to healing is more holistic. This is the way I rebuilt myself and have helped others to do the same. I believe that rather than just treating your symptoms, it's as important to dig deeper and treat the cause.

To get to the cause, it's necessary to look at you as a whole. Everything that happens in your body is a progression, so by looking at your entire story of illness, you can begin to see, from early symptoms, when and how things started.

If you get rid of one set of symptoms and don't treat the cause, your body will produce the same symptoms or another irritation somewhere else.

Here's an example:

I have a friend whose body was producing cancerous tumours very quickly. She had them removed but eventually her body could produce an apricot-sized tumour in the space of a month. Even she had to agree that there was only so much of her that could be cut out!

By now the cancer had her full attention. It made her sit up and start listening. She assessed where her life was out of balance, made changes and thankfully, is alive and well today.

The trouble is we've grown up believing symptoms are a nuisance, to be got rid of as quickly as possible, when actually they are the best way your body has of communicating with you. If your body could send you a text saying, 'Hey, your kidneys are struggling, we could use some help down here.' It would.

Instead, it responds with a symptom that will get your attention. Some pain and inflammation that releases or progresses, according to whether or not you listen and take action.

So you're saying symptoms are my body's way of communicating with me?

Absolutely.

Your body has one job and one job only. To keep you alive.

Your body has no interest in killing you. It will never actively attack you without reason. It will only attack something within you that it sees as foreign, or a threat. If this happens, you know something has gone seriously wrong, and this is never a simple or overnight process.

Too often, I hear people say, 'She just got cancer,' when I know this is impossible. In my experience and years of study and training, for everyone who suffers a major disease, there are symptoms years before. Clues and hints casually dropped by the body. Memos of pain and problems ignored until the body could cope no longer.

As far as your body is concerned, disease is a last resort.

Our troubles begin when we think we are smarter than the smartest piece of kit on the planet – our body! When we refuse to listen to our body, when we deny, or try and suppress our symptoms, then we leave the very cells that try to keep us alive, with no alternative. The simple fact is that our bodies create symptoms in response to the situation or circumstances they find themselves in. Who creates the situation or circumstances? Us.

So should we feel guilt, shame or blame about this? Hell, no!

Now that we have this information, should we do something about it? Hell, yes!

Of course, we can't be responsible for what may have been handed down to us through our family. That is part of our challenge and, I believe, what we're here to learn to overcome.

What we CAN BE responsible for is clearing out our toxicity and re-designing our lives so that anything other than health doesn't stand a chance. Everything we've experienced up until now is information. What matters is how we use this information to create something better.

So what should I do about my symptoms?

Honestly?

Start listening and paying attention.

Illness and disease in the body is ALWAYS a progression.

Look back at the development of your symptoms and use the information in this book to find the connections. Yes, this is a simplistic view of a complicated process, but the key is to understand that there are NO RANDOM EVENTS in the body.

Think about it this way:

If we suppress our symptoms, we add to the stress in the body and move towards illness. If we reduce stress and facilitate cleansing and release we unravel illness and move towards healing.

Stay with me on this one. The next bit of information could change your life!

So what are my symptoms telling me?

The most important message from your symptoms is the DIRECTION in which your health is heading.

To explain this, let me flip the work of a nineteenth-century doctor, Constantine Hering, on its head.

Hering formulated a law of cure which states that, when successfully treated, disease leaves the body in a certain way. I prefer to turn this process around to show how illness or disease progresses in the body in a certain way.

You can use this to understand how you got to this point in your health.

The progression of illness occurs like this:

1. **From bottom to top** – Symptoms generally start lower down in the body and work their way up as they become more serious. Look back through your health history, have your symptoms gradually moved higher?

2. **From outside to inside** – external conditions precede deeper conditions. So eczema (skin) manifests before asthma (lungs) and asthma before depression (mind). Have your symptoms have moved inwards, or deeper, over time?

3. **From lesser to greater organs** – All of our organs are important but if our liver is overloaded it is less life-threatening than a collapsed lung and likewise a collapsed lung is less life-threatening than a brain haemorrhage. So illness becomes more serious as it moves to more important organs. Check your worksheet and see which organs have been affected, and remember, your skin is an organ too!

That Seems Complicated!

Don't worry, all you need to remember is this – **Illness is a continuum of symptoms**.

Each symptom is your body asking for help.

If treatment allows your body to clear the toxicity then the problem or symptom disappears. This is how your body is designed to function.

However, if you treat a symptom but it doesn't clear the toxicity, either because it's not enough, or it suppresses the toxicity, then the symptom will persist or worsen and over time, move deeper and higher within the body.

Here's an example of this process:

Jane has infrequent bowel movements, suggesting her liver is overloaded and the residual toxicity is not being cleared through her congested bowels. Jane may experience symptoms such as discomfort, constipation, tiredness and general fatigue but she probably blames these on life in general.

Her body tries to find another solution. It uses its largest organ, the skin, to disperse the toxicity which creates eczema. This is the first symptom Jane really takes notice of.

Jane doesn't think about treating her bowel to clear the toxicity. Instead, she uses a steroid cream to get rid of the eczema.

The steroid cream may stop her itchy red skin but it doesn't allow the toxicity out. Even though it's used with the best of intentions, the steroid cream actually suppresses the toxicity and keeps it within the body.

Over time – remember everything is a progression – the toxicity moves deeper. In Jane, it manifests in the lungs as asthma.

Notice how symptoms have moved deeper into the body and higher up the body.

The asthma is considered in isolation and treated with inhalers. The bronchi in the lungs that are trying to repair themselves (thus creating a wheeze) are routinely forced open to allow Jane to breathe without the wheeze. The effect is that only minimal repair happens and release of the initial toxicity still isn't facilitated.

Again, over time, the toxicity moves higher and deeper again and in Jane it becomes depression, for which she is given more medication.

Can you see how toxicity has moved higher up and deeper within the body? Can you see that what really needs to happen is the release of toxicity?

Okay, this is one example of the progression of illness. Each person will react individually. You may see examples of acute episodes in your health history where toxicity was cleared and you moved towards health rather than towards illness.

This is why it's so important to evaluate your case history as a whole rather than as isolated episodes of illness with no relation to each other.

This is why it's important to be treated as an individual, rather than a series of symptoms.

I'm struggling to get my head around that

So did I initially, but when I went back through my case, I could see how my symptoms had progressed over time, becoming higher, deeper and more serious. As I healed, I could also see the reverse taking place as symptoms cleared up.

This process still helps me keep track of what's going on in my body. Now, when symptoms flare up, or have a chat with me ☺, I set about treating the cause to get fast and effective results so I move back towards health.

I know this is a holistic and possibly a new way of thinking about symptoms and how they're treated. Having experienced asthma I would never say that inhalers are a bad thing. It is very frightening when you can't breathe! Medication is essential in emergencies. I know, I've had appendicitis and two caesarean sections! However, if medication is to be used then it's very important to support the body throughout and still focus on treating the cause.

If you're looking back at your health history and stressing. Don't. The progression of illness happens over time, NOT overnight. We are all unique and so is the way our body will communicate via symptoms. The point is to become aware of how illness is created and this is why your worksheet, and your story, are like gold dust for you.

So how do I use all this information?

Well, folks, this is the fun part! This is where you get to piece your jigsaw puzzle together and make connections.

Start by looking back over the information in your worksheets.

Can you see where your symptoms or conditions have followed a progression and which way are your symptoms moving? From external and low down in your body to deeper and higher up?

Has illness targeted more important organs as it progressed?

If your symptoms seemed to clear but then a new and more serious symptom appeared, see if it was higher up, deeper, or concerned a more important organ than before. Or perhaps you suffered from a complaint affecting an organ for the first time.

Notice also if you had periods where symptoms cleared and you were well. Think about how you cleared this toxicity and if there was a particular trigger that caused it to re-emerge.

Spend some time over this to really get an overview of which direction your health is heading in. Keep the idea of progression in mind and build up a mine of information on how you've got to this point.

Now use the following explanation of the "Top to Toe Review" to add the final pieces to your jigsaw puzzle. Pick out the bits that are relevant for you. Try and link them to symptoms and see how the progression or regression of illness has occurred over time in your health story.

Top to Toe Review Explained

Refer back to your "Top to Toe" worksheet and use this to translate the message that your body is giving you.

It is by no means an exclusive or exhaustive list and it is not intended as a medical encyclopaedia. Rather it serves as a brief explanation of what symptoms can mean and how they are related to other parts of your body.

I found this helped clarify what was really going on in my body and provided a broad overview that was helpful in making sense of my symptoms.

Again, avoid the temptation to get caught up in the drama around any of these explanations and don't rush off to try and solve a particular problem. The following sections of this book provide the help you need to understand the nourishment and techniques you can use to calm and clear symptoms.

Some of the information below may strike you as irrelevant or unexpected. Roll with it. This is what I have learnt from years of study, application and experience personally and with clients. Theories from traditional Chinese medicine, for example, may seem "out there" but they come with thousands of years of practice and social proof.

When I was at my most ill, I was willing to try anything, and pretty much did. If you really want to rebuild your body and reclaim your life I urge you to become very open-minded about what might help you. There is no one path for us all to follow.

Do not worry if your symptoms have manifested differently to friends you know with the same condition. Some people are born with a lot of inherited toxicity so their symptoms are higher and deeper from the start and that's just the way it is. There is no right or wrong. We are all totally unique.

Refer back to your answers to your "Top to Toe Review" as you read the following and note down organs if they relate to your symptoms.

Concentration, Energy, Motivation

If any or all of your energy, motivation, concentration and memory ratings were low then this is likely to be linked to insufficient hydration and blood sugar issues.

Hair

Hair problems can be related to mineral depletion, an overloaded liver and low levels of essential fatty acids. All of these areas can be targeted through improved nutrition so if your hair is a problem then know that your current fuel is not doing enough for you.

Skin

Skin issues are usually indicative of bowel problems i.e. if your bowel is unable to clear toxicity or has become porous. The nutrition information in section 3 and the release techniques in section 5 will help.

Headaches / Migraines

Headaches and migraines are usually related to your liver. In a healthy body that experiences stress the liver is often the first organ to feel it and give us a symptom to let us know. The release techniques in section 5 will help.

Ear/ Nose / Throat

Nose and sinus problems are associated with dryness and are an indication that your bowel is dehydrated and struggling. Sinus problems can also show up before depression manifests.

Sore throats and tonsillitis are letting you know that your lymphatic system cannot clear the toxicity it's experiencing. If the lymphatic system is struggling then you know the liver is too.

Ear problems – In traditional Chinese medicine, ear problems are related to the kidneys which are said to be our "Jing" or source of energy. If your Jing is weak you may experience poor hearing or deafness. In Western medicine, ear infections are a sign that our lymphatic system is struggling and cannot move toxicity into the blood for clearing. Dehydration is also a factor here.

Chest / Lungs

In Chinese medicine, the lungs are the seat of grief and depression and they are usually linked to an earlier bowel or hydration issue. If you hear yourself sighing frequently, this is a sure sign of unresolved grief.

Stomach / Digestion

Eating the wrong foods and expecting the body to be able to digest them, or eating foods with little nutritional value that the body cannot create energy from, is a huge problem in our society. However, stress can also play a part and long-standing stomach issues can be a reflection of something in life that we find hard to stomach or digest. Eating disorders can also relate to self-worth issues.

Bowels

Bowels issues are related to hydration. Not just through water but also through essential fatty acids, or oils. When the intestine becomes dehydrated the mast cells in the colon produce histamine, which is the beginning of an allergic reaction.

Think of the drugs that are prescribed for allergies, they are anti-histamines. If you suffer from allergies your bowels are having a chat with you.

On an emotional level, if you have bowel issues consider what you are holding on to, or unable to let go of. A healthy bowel should empty every day, preferably once in the morning and once in the afternoon and stools should be firm and chocolate brown.

Urination

Urination problems relate to kidneys and bladder. There is likely to be dryness, inflammation and over acidity which may lead towards panic attacks if not resolved.

Legs and Below

Legs, knees, ankles are about moving forward with our lives.

Joint problems are usually related to acidity which in turn is linked to the liver and bowels being unable to excrete toxicity. The body tries to find a safe place to dump this toxicity and opts for the joints.

Feet problems usually show up as nail issues, warts or fungal infections which are all linked to the bowel and good gut flora.

How does this relate to my worksheet?

As you look through your worksheet notice how you have treated, or been treated for a condition and ask the following questions:

1. *Did the illness run its course and the symptoms disappear?*

2. *Was there a short-term improvement?*

3. *At a later time, did you experience new or different symptoms? If so, were they higher up or deeper in the body?*

4. *Which organs were involved?*

What you are looking for is Direction.

Have you been moving towards health or illness?

Do you have a high residual toxic load that shows up as chronic symptoms you've had for weeks, months, or even years?

Are you living in a coping strategy around your health?

Putting It All Together

Now it's time to put your "Top to Toe" information together with what you learned in your "The Story of You" worksheet.

As you work through your story and find out how you got to this point, notice which information jumps out at you, or resonates with you. Trust that this is most important right now.

Look back at each section of your "The Story of You" worksheet and answer the questions below.

Childhood

Consider your childhood. Was there anything significant in your childhood that increased your toxicity or allowed the release of toxicity? Perhaps you had a childhood illness that allowed your body to burn off toxicity?

I vividly remember a vibrant case of the mumps which left me bedridden for a few days but ultimately much stronger. This is the purpose of childhood illness.

As you look at your health story, notice if emotional or physical traumas or periods of unresolved stress were followed later by new symptoms. Again, if you can find the cause, you can use this information to assist your healing.

Bear in mind that everyone is different and will react differently and that is why it's important to work through this yourself before seeking outside counsel. Trust your intuition.

Puberty

What about puberty? What showed up for you during this time in your life? Was there any prolonged stress prior to your symptoms?

Did you experience a progression of symptoms that became more serious?

It's common for symptoms that manifest in puberty, if left unresolved, to re-appear in the twenties and thirties as something deeper and more insidious. See if this is the case for you. Can you find links between decades?

20s, 30s and beyond

Now look at the decades of your life.

If you are a woman who has had children, they are a good reflection of your state of health at the time. If it was easy to conceive and you sailed through pregnancy with few symptoms and had a problem free (notice I didn't say pain-free) natural birth, your body was in very good shape.

If you struggled to conceive, suffered morning sickness and fatigue and were overdue, or had a long hard labour or required a C-section, your body probably needed more preparation. See if you can identify any imbalances.

Post childbirth is also very telling. How quickly we bounce back, how much milk we have to breastfeed, all indicate the state of our health. If you are someone who had numerous children in quick succession, were there symptoms that arose later as a result of such an emotionally and physically demanding time?

Regardless of whether you are male or female, look at your state of health through each decade and whether symptoms improved or deteriorated.

Are there any symptoms that disappeared completely and then perhaps something deeper occurred several months or perhaps a year later?

Did you take medication for a symptom to find it disappeared but then discovered a new symptom elsewhere?

Try and make connections to see in which direction things are moving. Get an idea of how your state of health has changed and developed over your lifetime.

Factor your work into the equation of your health. Your sense of purpose is largely affected by the sense of service and reward you experience through work. Whether this is a job as the world understands it, or raising kids, volunteering etc.

If you have been able to be part of a fulfilling work or enterprise how has this affected your health?

Are there periods when you wanted to work but were unable to?

Can you see a correlation in your health picture or symptoms?

What about a job change or redundancy? Don't underestimate the stress this places on our bodies. Factor this into your health history.

I need help with this!

No problem, reach out to me on Facebook so I can help you make connections.

Okay, I'm beginning to see what's happened but now what do I do?

Firstly, try and re-connect your mind with your body. I know when I was ill, I lost all faith in my ability to be well and you may feel the same. If you've developed an inherent distrust of your body then now is the time to change. My hope is that once you stop seeing your symptoms in isolation, you can rebuild that trust and take action.

Know that if you support your body, it will always support you.

Use the knowledge and insights you have gained about your past to create your future. The faster you listen and take action, the quicker your rebuild to great health will be.

You cannot change something until you accept it.

Accept where you are in your health right now. Stop fighting or resisting and understand that this is the perfect place from which to learn and rebuild yourself. The point of power is always within you.

Should I go to my doctor?

Resist the temptation to run to your doctor, expecting him or her to marvel at these connections. I can only speak from experience when I say this approach didn't work for me. Thankfully, times are changing and many doctors now recognise that a more holistic approach is beneficial and in some cases, can complement an allopathic approach, but right now, this information is for you.

Let me be very clear. I'm not saying everything you've been told by doctors is wrong. I'm offering you information which I hope will help you make sense of what's happened to your health and provide another avenue to explore, if you're frustrated or not getting the results you want from conventional medicine.

This is an opportunity to see things differently. To create the space for you to take responsibility for your health, from wherever you are right now.

Take the time to sit with this process of discovery for a while and let yourself finish the work. Get as much of your story recorded as possible and be prepared for more revelations and insights to come.

I'm worried about my family history of...

Don't.

Worry is another word for stress and all stress creates is dehydration and illness. The fact is, we all have a history of something and if we've had kids we've likely handed stuff down. It's part of life and we're learning and evolving.

This is not the time to invest your valuable energy in the blame game. It serves no purpose. If you're looking at your ancestry and wailing, 'Oh, my God, there's two generations of diabetes in my family, of course, I'm going to get it,' take a breath. The only person who gets to decide your symptoms, conditions and diseases, is YOU.

See it this way. If you haven't had kids and you intend to, then doing this work and following this process will help you offload some toxicity. If you have kids and they have health issues then you can rebuild yourself and pay it forward by teaching them to do the same. There's always your grandkids to think about ☺ And why stop there? If this works for you, tell your friends, let them benefit too.

My vision is a world where everyone's responsible for their own health, actively creating vitality and balance.

Have I been doing everything wrong?

No.

My aim is not to invalidate everything you may have been told about your health so far. You've done the best you could with the information that was available to you. That's all any of us can do!

Right now my aim is to give you NEW information to help you evaluate, understand and change your health, forever. If this approach contradicts what you think you know, then stay open to seeing things differently. If your health has stagnated around a picture of illness or symptoms that refuse to budge, then maybe it's time for a shift.

If you're tempted to start judging yourself, the health professionals who have treated you, or anyone else you're holding responsible, I have one word for you.

DON'T.

There's a mountain of work out there that unequivocally tells us blame and guilt do us no good. They are another form of resentment and resentment makes us ill. I'll show you how to deal with these feelings in sections 7 and 8

Should I stop taking my medication?

No. Remember it's taken you weeks, months, or even years to get to this point. It will take a while to unravel ill-health and support yourself into vitality. Drastic action creates drastic results and it is essential that you prepare your body before asking it to release. Most importantly, you need to know how to support it WHILE it is releasing. This is covered in section 5.

When you become stronger and experience tangible results, then it's time to talk to your healthcare provider and use your judgement about weaning yourself off medication.

Can I trust my doctor to support me in this?

My advice is, if you can't talk to your doctor about supporting yourself through illness, or they cannot see you beyond your current state of illness, then it's time to find a new doctor.

What's next?

Now's your chance to own your health story, without blame, shame or judgement. Yes, this is how you got here. There it is, all your stuff laid out on a worksheet, hopefully with some connections.

To clear anything from our system and our psyche, we first have to witness it. You're doing that right now. Choose to let it empower you. Choose to let it inform the decisions you make about your health from this point forward. You're here because you're meant to be here. You're reading this book because you're ready to get better.

Before we jump into section 3, I'd like you to make a clear stand for the issue you want to address. Right now, note down the biggest health issue that jumps out at you from the work you just completed.

Mark this clearly – the health problem or issue I want to address is:

Journal Space

SECTION 3

YOUR FUEL
ASSESSMENT

I'd been working on my rebuild for about five years before I really took nutrition seriously. I'd cut a lot of stressful ingredients out of my diet, which I'll take you through shortly, but I was only focussing on avoiding food that created a reaction in me. That left me eating a very uninspiring diet which felt like deprivation.

I was stuck at the level of managing my symptoms but not really seeing a big health improvement beyond that. I hadn't grasped the concept of food as the fuel of my rebuild. It was only when I happened to listen to a free nutrition lecture that a light bulb went on. I realised that if I wanted to do more than cope with my symptoms, I needed to address how I was nourishing myself.

The nutrition lecture turned out to be a turning point in my life. The information resonated with me. I could see myself in so many of the cases that were discussed and I could apply what I learnt immediately. Over two years, I trained and certified as a Natural Nutritionist and began to help other people with health problems as well as myself.

One of the key concepts I learnt is that any structure is only as strong as its foundations and while I could pull off looking healthy, if I was put under any stress, I'd be straight back to bed for a lie-down. My foundations were shaky!

In this section, you'll go through a "Fuel assessment" to discover whether you're nourishing yourself or creating more stress. Sometimes even our best intentions and everything we've been taught are consciously or subconsciously adding to our toxicity.

Toxic Fuel

This is the traditional food pyramid, promoted as a healthy eating model in the 1990s. Turns out it's anything but!

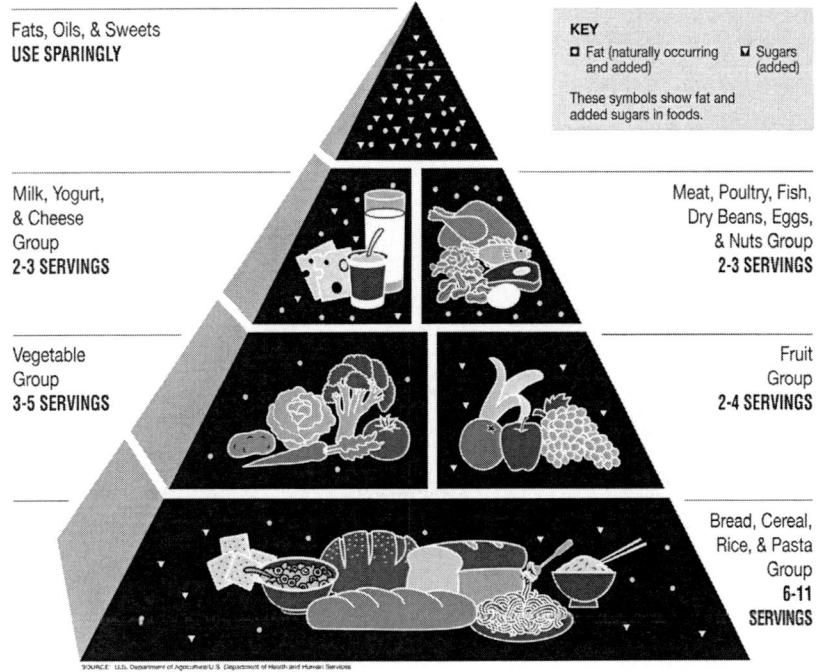

Source: US Department of Agriculture. Food, Nutrition, and Consumer Services. Center for Nutrition Policy and Promotion. (Wikimedia Commons)

Chances are, you've seen this pyramid before. For years, this model was promoted as the means to create health. It was displayed in classrooms and hung proudly on the walls of doctor's waiting rooms and many people took it to heart.

In reality, an over-reliance on carbohydrates has produced obesity and diabetes. The truth is, if you eat according to the food pyramid model, you'll probably end up looking like the food pyramid!

There are a lot of confused, overweight and depressed people out there as a result of these guidelines. If you're one of them, or you find yourself baffled by the latest science and conflicting reports in the media about what you should eat, then you'll love this section. I'm going to give you simple answers and an easy to follow "ADD and AVOID" plan which you can use straight away.

For every input there's an effect

Let's go back to basics. The point of eating and drinking is to provide the body with energy to keep us going and repair us as needed, but not all energy is created equal.

I have been blessed to have many teachers along my journey to health, but one of them had a saying that sticks with me to this day:

For every input, there's an effect.

You know this from your personal experience. Can you remember a time when you've over-eaten or under-eaten? Either situation can make you feel lousy. And who hasn't suffered the most common effect of excess alcohol, a hangover?

Or perhaps you had a difficult day. A relationship ended and left you an emotional wreck, and for the next two days you felt awful. Drained and exhausted, as though you were coming down with something. The end of the relationship was the input, the resulting fatigue and immune response was the effect.

Nothing happens by chance in the body.

The input that had the greatest effect on me was white cane sugar. The processed stuff that a 2007 research study*[*] found to be more addictive than cocaine. During my worst days, I was so weak I craved it and yet I only had to have a tiny amount to feel off-balance and ready to pass out within a matter of minutes.

If you can relate to this, or know of foods or beverages that create a definite adverse reaction in you, note them down.

Foods/ beverages or substances that create a definite adverse reaction in me are:

* Source:http://articles.mercola.com/sites/articles/archive/2007/08/23/is-sugar-more-addictive-than-cocaine.aspx

Consider when, how and why you choose to consume this food or drink.

I consume this food/beverage/substance because it makes me feel

How often do you indulge?

How long does it take for the reaction to occur?

How long does it take you to recover and feel well/normal again?

Think of your body as a Formula One car for a moment. Give it the right fuel and it will roar around the track, full of energy. Fill it with dirty water and – well, you get the picture.

If you are committed to making a change and nourishing yourself, sign below.

Sign here………………….

Date………………

But I love… (insert the input that creates your effect).

Me too. I LOVED sugar! I mean REALLY LOVED it!!!

For you it might be cake or bread, or perhaps you can't stay off fast food. This isn't an accident. Anything loaded with sugar, fat and salt, or a heady combination of the three, is likely to become highly addictive.

Research shows food companies pump sugar, fat and salt into their products in order to hit what science calls, your "Bliss" point. The point you can't say, 'NO!'

The "Bliss" point is a chemical reaction that triggers a feeling you want to experience again and again. You think you LOVE it, but your body is screaming, 'HELP ME!'

What's your most toxic input?

Side-effects

If you have ever taken any form of medication you will have been warned about the possible "side-effects". These are the unwanted reactions that might occur. Yet if you've glugged your way through several cans of soda or munched on a Big Mac, the "side-effects" probably never crossed your mind.

Here's the truth. There are no such things as "side-effects", there are only EFFECTS. An input creates an effect and a "side-effect" is an effect. Period.

There's a universal law of cause and effect in our lives, which basically means that, for everything we put into our body, be it food, drink, or our own thoughts, there's a reaction. Boy, did I learn this the hard way.

If this is where you are right now, consider Dale Carnegie's words in his book *How to Win Friends and Influence People*:

> **'By becoming interested in the cause, we are less likely to dislike the effect.'**

In other words, when you understand the effect you're creating, you'll choose more carefully!

Are you ready to make better choices?

What Do You Want More Of?

So the decision you have to make is really simple. What do you want more, health or the food/beverage/substance that's keeping you stuck in illness?

However much I loved sugar, I had to stop seeing it as a treat, an indulgence or a pleasure. I learnt to look it square in the eye and say 'I choose me, instead'.

As part of my rebuild I gave up sugar – and I mean anything with sugar in it – for two years. I became the biggest label checker in history and found sugar in all kinds of products – even bread!

Why does anyone need sugar in bread?

Initially, my shopping trips were long and tedious (this was before Wholefoods and other fabulous health shops) but I soon savvied up and realised there were whole aisles I could avoid. Anything packaged or processed tended to have sugar in it and I just stopped shopping those sections of the supermarket.

It wasn't that I didn't want the cake, cookies, crisps etc. It was that I didn't want the effect they would cause. I didn't want the output. I only wanted to input what would make me feel better and the more I nourished myself the better I felt. Over time, as I stopped shopping the "sugar" aisles as I called them, I started to forget about the products I used to crave. When I did come across them, it was easy to carry on walking as I didn't even recognise them as food any more.

If you're someone who's lived on fast or processed food, then you can expect a corresponding effect or output. If you're living with this output on a daily basis then you'll see that your current state of health is a reflection of this.

Today is your opportunity to start making better choices. Your first one was reading this book ☺

If you think you're healthy but you're still frustrated with your lack of results then this next exercise might shed some light for you.

The message is clear: change your fuel, change your life.

Fill in your "Fuel Assessment" chart on the next page. Copy, or make your own version for each week and most importantly. START TODAY. Even if it's a Wednesday. Just start. ☺

This is an assessment of the fuel you're putting in.

Don't judge or be dishonest and don't feel the need to share this information. The only person who needs to see this right now is you. This means you can be realistic. If you're starving yourself, denying yourself or overindulging, own it.

This is where all cheating stops.

Note down all food and drink for a typical day. If you find yourself eating really well on day one, that's fine. You'll soon slip into your normal eating pattern. Keep filling out the sheets and accept where you currently are with your nutrition. Remember witnessing a problem is the first step in resolving it.

The process of rebuilding requires clearing out, starting over and seeing yourself in a different light. Look back on this page in three months, six months, or a year and see how far you have come.

The power to change exists in any given moment and it is all yours.

	Before Breakfast	Breakfast	Snack
Day One			
Day Two			
Day Three			
Day Four			
Day Five			
Day Six			
Day Seven			

Midday Meal	Snack	Evening Meal	Snack/Extras

Help Re-Fuelling

So now you have an idea of what you're putting in. Make sure you noted down beverages as well as food consumed. Hydration is a key part of your recovery.

As you take a look at your fuel assessment chart consider the following. Do you wake up hungry or are you mistaking hunger for thirst?

Are you eating before you feel hungry?

Is the first thing you eat or drink loaded with sugar or caffeine? Either will get your nerves jangling, put stress on your system and leave you hungry and dissatisfied. It's a downward spiral from there.

Are you nourishing or toxifying?

Are you skipping breakfast because you don't have time?

A bit on breakfast

You've probably heard the saying "breakfast is the most important meal of the day". If you're rebuilding yourself this almost certainly rings true and here's why.

Breakfast is your opportunity to stabilise your blood sugar. I was taught that if I had a good protein breakfast, before 8am, my blood sugar would be stable for the rest of the day. This proved to be right and when I started managing my breakfast properly, years of roller-coastering between energy and lethargy disappeared and I stopped reaching for the snack tin by 10am and falling asleep at 11am.

In traditional Chinese medicine, the largest meal of the day is eaten at breakfast because this is when digestive powers are said to be at their strongest. My best days are when I have a large meal for breakfast, usually last night's leftover meat and vegetables. Yes, it can feel weird to eat meat and veg at 8am at first, but it feels great to be energised and without a whimper of hunger until midday.

Using the nourishment plan, I'll teach you, I stabilised my blood sugar in just over a week. Yep, it wasn't that hard, I just needed to know what to do. My ADD and AVOID plan changed my life and it can help you too.

But I'm not hungry at breakfast time

Okay, if you're genuinely not hungry then there's no need to force food down first thing. A drink is important though as it maintains hydration. A warm drink is even better as it stimulates the bowels. For me, a cup of nettle tea never fails – and it's strangely tasty ☺

Have a drink and then wait until you are hungry, just don't let yourself go hungry. If being overweight is part of your health problem then some gentle exercise can be a great way to get your system moving before you eat. If you can't manage a walk in the fresh air and you're not hungry, try some simple stretching or yoga.

Lunch or no time to munch?

What about lunch? Are you skipping it and then reaching for snacks as your blood sugar dives mid-afternoon?

Or are you eating a good lunch but still suffering a food "coma" afterwards because your digestive system isn't strong enough to cope and it really needs you to take a nap while it tries to do its job? For years, I had to have a power nap, which should have been fifteen minutes but actually lasted one hour. My body simply didn't have the energy to digest food AND keeping me awake and moving around.

If you're stuck in the vicious cycle of sugar highs and lows then rather than eating a large lunch, break it down into two smaller meals and have the first around 11am and the second around 2pm. This helps to ensure a consistent supply of energy.

If you feel sluggish after eating try switching to a macrobiotic approach where protein and carbohydrates are eaten separately, making it easier for the digestive system.

I eat on the hoof because of work

Look at when you're eating and whether you're really nourishing yourself.

Grazing (eating little and often throughout the day) does suit some people. It can reduce the digestive load and help balance your blood sugar, by stopping a sugar low. As long as what you eat is nourishing and not stressful for your system. If it results in one long snacking process of junk and more junk then it's increasing your toxicity.

Note the times of your meals. Are they well staggered throughout the day or do you grab a bit for breakfast, skimp on lunch or skip it entirely and then eat a big meal late at night when your digestion has pretty much clocked off for the day?

If you're literally eating on the run, or as you're moving around, then you are increasing the challenge factor on your digestive system. Our bodies respond to our interaction with food. When we look at food and engage with food, our brain sends a message for the correct digestive enzymes to be produced to digest it. As we savour the food, chewing properly, swallowing and enjoying the experience then our body should be in the optimal state to absorb nutrients.

If you are barely paying attention to food, don't be surprised if you glean only the minimal nutritional value from it.

What about my night-time nibble habit?

Do you find yourself rooting through the cupboard late in the evening?

What's the snack you turn to? Is it genuine hunger or a lack of something in your life that you're trying to fill with ice cream, buttered toast, or as it used to be in my case, mature cheddar?

Obviously, I can't see you. I don't know if daytime snacking and eating at night are good things for your size, shape and health, but instinctively, you do. Trust in your ability to make corrections. That's what owning your health means. Use my basic plan to rebuild and get out of your "health hole". Then when your energy picks up, explore new ways of eating and begin to enjoy the process.

I'm really worried about my fuel assessment

Don't be. You've done the archaeological dig. The research into how you got to this point now. Now it's time to do the fun stuff. This is the architectural part, where you begin to create the new, healthy you.

If it seems like a herculean task, don't be overwhelmed. Implement this at your pace, with a kind heart and an attitude of self-love that wants health, instead of the cookie jar.

Resist overwhelm or confusion. These are avoidance strategies that stop you moving forward and we'll tackle those in sections 7 and 8. Your potential for health is far greater than your resistance to it. Be pulled by the body and health you want as much as you are pushed by not wanting what you see and feel in your body now.

This is the blueprint for your rebuild. It's a process. I wasn't a minor renovation, I was a knock down and start from scratch. If this is where you are, know that what is possible for one is possible for all.

What About Water?

How's your water intake?

For some people, water doesn't even come into the equation. It's one long round of soda, caffeine and juice. I've heard many people complain that they "can't do water", which always seems strange given that our bodies are made up of around 70% water.

No, I really can't do water

You don't have to DO water, you ARE water. Your health and hydration are intrinsically linked, but of course you are free to choose and ill health is the alternative. I won't labour this point. There's enough information in the public sphere to fill a library but if you'd like a recommendation which explains why water is so fundamental to our existence, try this book: *Your Body's Many Cries for Water* by Dr F Batmanghelidj.

It clearly shows the correlation between hydration and health and you can find it on the Rebuild Library page of the website.

Still in denial?

Here's what you need to know:

Caffeine, soda, alcohol, juice should not be seen as "hydration". They do not have the same effect.

When you become dehydrated, your body puts a protective barrier around your cells. This barrier is a cholesterol membrane which protects all the good stuff inside (think DNA and the very building blocks of you). This membrane protects the contents of your cells but it also keeps toxins trapped inside as the nightly detox process can't happen. Many argue that this build-up of toxicity in the cells is the beginning of all disease.

In a dehydrated state, you quickly lose your mental clarity. Your ability to think clearly, to reason and make decisions. If you find yourself in this state on a regular basis or if you experience brain fog, try sipping water frequently.

In traditional Chinese medicine, we are made up of elements and it is the water element within us that holds fear and anxiety. If you are dehydrated you will feel stressed and fearful. If you are constantly anxious and agitated, rehydration is a very simple self-help tool. Use it.

What if I don't drink much and I don't feel dehydrated?

Everyday dehydration isn't always easy to recognise or necessarily associate with a lack of water. Check through the list of symptoms below to see if you experience any of them on a regular basis.

Symptoms of mild dehydration:

- *Tiredness*

- *Headaches*

- *Migraines*

- *Sinus problems*

- *Dry skin*

- *Bad breath*

- *Muscle cramps*

- *Food cravings (especially for sweet stuff)*

- *Irritability or confusion*

- *Light-headedness.*

If you think mild dehydration just affects your mood and energy, think again. It can also contribute to:

Kidney stones, liver, joint and muscle damage including heart problems, high cholesterol, blood pressure problems, constipation…the list goes on.

If you haven't been hydrating for a while, you're probably used to being in a dehydrated state. Your body will have adopted a coping strategy. Try increasing your water intake over the next 3–5 days and see if you notice a difference.

Be prepared that your body may try to hold on to water initially in a "Hooray! Finally a decent drink" mode, but it will adjust and you should quickly experience the benefits.

To work out how much water you need, take your body weight in kilogrammes and multiply it by 0.033. This will give you the ideal amount of water in litres per day for you. If it's more than you are currently drinking work up to it **gradually**.

What about fruit juice and fizzy drinks?

If you have a blood sugar issue i.e. you find yourself getting tired, fuzzy-headed and reaching for a biscuit mid-morning or mid-afternoon, then my advice is, stay away from sugary drinks.

Vegetable juices, especially those with leafy greens are better than fruit juices, as they tend to be less sweet and more nourishing.

Flavoured waters have become very popular but check the sugar content. If it's sugar by any other name then steer clear.

Fizzy drinks, pop or soda are a complete NO. Did you know just 1 can of Coke contains nine teaspoons of sugar!

What about diet sodas / drinks?

They sound good but they're not. They are addictive, and most worryingly, studies show they can actually increase weight gain not reduce it*.

How?

Artificial sweeteners are hundreds of times sweeter than real sugar. So when consumed, your body thinks masses of sugar has been ingested. Your body produces insulin, but because no real sugar has been ingested the insulin is not needed and instead gets laid down to belly fat.

The result? Diabetes and obesity.

If you think diet drinks are "filling you up", think again. You're not ingesting food or nourishment. You're consuming a sugar high. Research shows people who drink soda end up more hungry and eat more as a result.

Here are some results from a fourteen-year study that Dr Mark Hyman cites in his brilliant book, *The Blood Sugar Solution 10-Day Detox Diet*.

> *'Diet sodas raised the risk of diabetes more than sugar sweetened sodas.'*

> *'Women who drank diet sodas drank twice as much as those who drank sugar sweetened sodas because artificial sweeteners are more addictive than regular sugar.'*

If you look on a map, obesity rates correlate around the world with per head consumption of soda. The message? Don't drink soda or diet soda, and unless you want to create sugar addicts, don't give it to your kids.

Okay, I hear you, but I really can't stand water

I believe you. I've met people who can't even bear to sip on a bottle of the stuff.

When I was in denial about what I could and couldn't do, one of my great teachers, Mary Morrissey, helped me get clear on what I was choosing. She said:

> *'You can have your reasons, or you can have results.'*

Turns out I wanted results more than I wanted my reasons.

I get that water may not appear the most interesting drink, so don't think of it as a drink. Think of it as a lifesaver. To make water more interesting start creating your own infusions. Add cucumber, mint or chunks of fresh or frozen fruit and let the flavours steep into the water. In summer, you can also make regular fruit tea and add ice to create a refreshing iced tea.

How Else Can I Hydrate?

If drinking water is going to require some work or some re-training then increase your consumption of foods that already hold water to boost your hydration. In other words, get water from food.

Cucumber and watermelon are obvious picks but here's also cantaloupe, strawberries, celery, lettuce, zucchini or courgette, leafy greens, tomatoes and bell peppers.

You can also use foods that absorb water as they're cooked. Quinoa and short grain brown rice are good examples. With short grain brown rice you can simmer it for far longer than necessary to actually cook it and just keep adding water.

My Little Miracle

I have a little secret that boosted my hydration and helped to stabilise my blood sugar. It's a recipe that's beautifully simple and yet highly effective in treating a variety of conditions from constipation to allergies.

I'll warn you now, you may not like the look of it, so before we get that far, let me tell you how fabulous it is. I recommended it to a man suffering with an ugly red rash that started as an allergic reaction to some chemicals he'd been using. The rash spread across his face and neck and became unbearably painful. He used the recipe I'm about to share with you and in 24hrs the rash, and the discomfort, had gone.

Another client baulked when I gave him some, but when he relented and started using it regularly, his anxiety attacks quickly diminished and he started coping with life much better.

What am I talking about? Is it some expensive product, that's difficult to find? Nope, not even close. It's something I learnt about when I trained to become a nutritionist and I've given it to many people, with fabulous results. It's called Linseed tea and you can make it easily in your kitchen. Here's the recipe.

Recipe for Linseed Tea

(Note – linseeds are the seeds of the flax plant so in your part of the world they may be called flaxseeds).

4 tablespoons brown linseeds to every 2 litre / 2qt of water – the amount of water doesn't have to be exact. If you use less water the consistency is thicker. You can adjust it to your taste, or as I like to call it, gloop preference!

Put the linseeds and the water in a saucepan and bring to the boil. Then turn off the heat, cover and leave it to stand for approx. 12hrs. You don't need to set your stopwatch for this. I tend to make mine before bed and leave it overnight.

Bring it back to the boil and let it simmer for 1hr. Allow it to cool slightly then pass it through a sieve to separate the seeds and the liquid. If you leave it until it's completely cool you may find it's too thick to sieve. Even when it's still warm the liquid may be thick and gloopy. This is because the natural oils in the seeds have worked their way out into the water and this is what makes it so fabulous for your health. This liquid constitutes linseed tea and it is full of the essential fatty acids that many of us are deficient in.

How to use it

To make linseed tea, fill a mug or cup about 1/3rd full with the linseed tea mixture, then dilute with 2/3rds hot water.

Let me give you a heads up – the tea mixture looks (and acts) like unset brown jello/jelly (I've actually chased mine across the kitchen work surface once when it tried to escape) – but HERE'S THE GOOD NEWS – it doesn't smell or taste of anything other than a mild black tea.

If you don't like the taste, you can add a slice of lemon, a bit of honey or even a herbal teabag and then you're ready to drink. Be creative!

Why is it so fabulous?

It provides essential fatty acids, or more specifically omega 3s, in a food form that our bodies can use straight away. This isn't an engineered tablet that your liver has to figure out what to do with. You don't need to take a lecithin supplement with it to ensure your body can use it.

It's ready to go and your body will thank you. I know people who've used linseed tea to treat all kinds of skin complaints with great results.

Why should I try it?

Many people are dehydrated without even knowing it. You may be drinking enough water but you also need to hydrate with oils and this is what the linseeds provide. Our modern diets in the developed world tend to be heavy on the omega 6 fatty acids, leaving most people short on omega 3s and we need both to be healthy.

What else do I need to know?

A great time to drink linseed tea is in between meals. Particularly, if you want to balance your blood sugar.

Once cool you should keep the linseed tea in the fridge. It will last for 2–3 days.

Add and Avoid: A Simple Long-Term Plan

This is a very simple chapter, because contrary to what a lot of people think, eating to create health does not need to be complicated. I use two lists, one list of foods to AVOID and another list of foods to ADD in their place.

As you look through the list your reaction might be, 'What! I can't have biscuits anymore???'

It's really important to re-frame this for yourself. Sure you may not have biscuits for a while, but if you had more energy instead wouldn't that be a good thing? Hold fast to the picture of health that you want to create. I'll show you how to do this in section 7.

If you feel tempted by something (for me it's always something sugary) support yourself by not shopping that aisle. Imagine if you don't walk down the biscuits aisle how hard it will be for your usual pack to accidentally "fall" into your trolley.

If this is going to be tricky for you, the hardest part will be the first few days, while your body still expects the usual food. Make sure you have the new foods stocked up and you have something to distract you. A warm drink, a walk, a phone call, something inspirational on the Rebuild Your Health Youtube channel or anything that takes your mind off the craving for 15–20 minutes is a helpful tool.

Use the Action sheet on the following page to plan and keep track of your choices. Copy or make your own version for each week.

Start by deciding to cut out one "avoid" food for this week. Write down which food you will not be having and stick to it.

Then write down the food or foods you'll be adding in its place. Each week put another avoid food on your list until you're avoiding all stressful foods and nourishing yourself with food that makes you feel good.

Notice how you feel each week. Pay attention to your energy levels and moods. Be conscious that by removing these stressful foods you are allowing your body to cleanse and supporting it in rebuilding.

Food to Avoid

Week 1	Week 2	Week 3	Week 4

Drink to Avoid

Week 1	Week 2	Week 3	Week 4

Food to Add

Week 1	Week 2	Week 3	Week 4

Drink to Add

Week 1	Week 2	Week 3	Week 4

Foods to Avoid

Sugar

Especially high fructose corn syrup, or glucose corn syrup, the sweetener used in most processed foods.

Sugar products

Molasses, liquid sugar like soda, bottled drinks, fruit juices.

Dairy

Milk, sweetened, flavoured yoghurt and yoghurt drinks and ice cream are the big ones.

Caffeine

Alcohol

Wheat

Damaged fats

1. margarine
2. hydrogenated oils. Start checking ingredient lists.

Crisps

Anything laden with flavours, preservatives and sweeteners canned food

Processed food

Red meat

I'm blood type O and always feel better for red meat. However, red meat isn't easy to digest and if your system is sluggish it may only add extra stress, so it's better to avoid it until you feel stronger.

But the AVOID list is full of my favourite foods!

You may think so right now but I guarantee your body does not love them in the same way you do.

Look back at your fuel assessment chart. How many of these AVOID foods regularly feature?

Notice how you feel after eating them?

Is there a food that causes bloating or gives you wind?

Is there something that makes you sleepy and lethargic, or grumpy and agitated? Start by avoiding those first.

Why no milk?

It's said that by the time we're around four years old most of us are no longer synthesizing the right enzymes to be able to digest the lactose in milk. Many of us continue to consume it but this can become stressful for the body. If you're worrying about calcium, don't. There are far better sources of calcium available (leafy greens for example).

Do I have to cut out ALL of the Avoid list?

That depends on how much better you want to feel. It all comes down to choice and you have to choose whether you want to be well or not.

If you don't nourish yourself there's no pill that can do it for you. If you're eating a poor diet and popping vitamin pills in the hope that they'll offset your eating, with all the love in the world, you're kidding yourself.

The bottom line is – if you're eating junk food, you're effectively starving yourself. Your body needs nutrition in a recognisable and usable format.

I started by cutting out sugar and saw an immediate change in my energy levels, so I went on to cut out all of the AVOID list. It's important to state here, that nobody forced me to. I did it because I wanted, or rather, needed, to feel better as fast as possible.

You can manage this at your pace according to how well you want to feel. Just know that the more change you create the more shift in your health you are likely to experience.

Remember: Anything in the AVOID column may taste fantastic to you because it probably contains the sugar/fat/salt combination which quickly has you addicted. BUT, while it tastes good, to your liver and other internal organs, it's more stress to deal with.

So what should I be eating?

Simple foods that aid cleansing and detoxing thereby encouraging healing. Here is your ADD list right alongside the AVOID so you can see how to make substitutions in your diet.

Foods to ADD

Avoid	Add
Sugar	Look for naturally sweet fruits and veg when you need that sweet kick. In cooking, I use small amounts of 100% natural maple syrup.
Caffeine	Herbal tea. Linseed tea. Water.
Alcohol	Sparkling water infused with fruit.
	Kombucha.
Wheat	I use Rye bread or Spelt bread. Many of the "wheat free" breads in the supermarkets are too rubbery, or full of ingredients, I don't recognise so I steer clear.
	For pasta, I use corn, rice or spelt. Rice noodles are particularly good in terms of taste and texture. I also use short grain brown rice instead of pasta as I can cook it for an hour and let it absorb lots of water.
	For flour, I use rice, almond or buckwheat.
	Instead of sugary cereal for breakfast I have oats or oat bran made into porridge.
	For couscous, I use quinoa which is delicious and easy to prepare.
Damaged Fats	Butter instead of margarine and use in moderation.
	Unheated olive oil on salad.
	Coconut oil or ghee to cook with as both are safe to heat.

Avoid	Add
Crisps	Vegetable crisps in un-hydrogenated oil. Seaweed snacks. I love the Itsu Wasabi seaweed snacks. Nuts.
Milk	There are several alternatives now. Almond is my favourite. Soy my least favourite as it is a known goitrogen which means it suppresses thyroid function.
	If you like yoghurt, avoid low fat or sweetened/flavoured in favour of plain, full fat, unsweetened organic yoghurt. Because yoghurt is fermented, it is easier for our bodies to digest. A Harvard study found one 28g serving of yoghurt every day lowers the risk of type 2 diabetes. (Source BMC MED, 2014;12:215) Add a bit of fruit, maple syrup or honey to sweeten.
Canned Food	Fresh meat, fish and vegetables plus fruit in moderation. You will be amazed how much better you feel if you keep it simple. Vegetables are your main alkalisers so eat plenty. See the list in "Additional Adds".
Processed Food	Fresh meat, fish and vegetables as above.
	Instead of processed snacks that are loaded with flavours, preservatives, sugar and salt go for nuts, seeds, fruit and raw vegetable crudités.
Red Meat	Chicken (organic where possible). Deepwater fish like salmon, cod and halibut are excellent.

ADDITIONAL ADDS

Protein powders

I use hemp but there's a variety available so check out what's available at your health store and see what you prefer. These are a great way to boost your protein intake at breakfast. Other good protein breakfast choices are eggs, nuts, hummus, meat, and fish.

Vegetables

If you like potatoes, use sweet instead of white potatoes and go easy on them as they are starchy carbohydrates. Make it interesting by using a range of colours, shapes and textures. If you have a lot of inflammation (which you'll experience as pain) go for brightly coloured vegetables, leafy greens and broccoli as these all reduce inflammation.

Vegetables really are an essential part of your Rebuild. A recent study shows that people who don't eat enough fruits and vegetables are far more likely to suffer "low mental wellbeing" which is linked to mental illness and depression. (Source WDDTY Dec 2014)

Consume vegetables high in phytonutrients that have special detoxifying chemicals in them. Broccoli, cabbage, cauliflower, kale, onion and bok choy are all good examples.

Fruits

Make berries your best friend, especially blueberries and raspberries. Cherries and apples are also good and only eat bananas or any really sweet fruit in moderation.

Whole grains

Researchers from Harvard University did a 24-year study and found that a daily serving of 28g of whole grains decreases the risk of cardiovascular death by 9% and premature death by 5%.

Seeds

Chia, pumpkin, hemp, flaxseeds.

Nuts

Nuts are a great snack. Use them to improve your metabolism and boost your protein intake. Opt for Brazil, walnut, almonds, pecans and macadamias.

Supplements

I tried a variety of supplements during my rebuild and even had vitamin injections. I do think it's worthwhile taking a good (unsweetened, non-dairy) probiotic and a multi-vitamin tablet. How much of either you can absorb really depends on your state of health but taken for 5 days, with 2 days off, I think it's a back-up plan that's worth investing in. If you try this for a month and see no difference then give it a rest. There's no point wasting money.

I don't like any of the "ADD" stuff.

You don't like it or maybe you've never really given it a chance?

Take out the junk and you'll find your palate changing. You'll be able to notice subtle flavours and textures. See this as an experiment. Take time over it. Keep an open mind. If you can't get excited about it from a taste perspective, get excited about it from a feeling better perspective.

Remember, it's a question of input versus effect.

Is there a way to rebuild without using the AVOID list?

Yes – Very slowly! How long have you got?

Or more importantly, how long you want to stay in your current state of health? The bottom line is this: If your body's trying to use food that is difficult to process, then it's wasting a lot of energy that could be directed to your repair and rebuild instead.

The purpose of the "AVOID" column is to take the stress off your body. A helpful way to look at toxic food is by the response it creates in your body. If you're eating something processed, unnatural, or in a form that barely resembles food – cheese in a tube anyone? – Then this creates stress in your body. If your system is stressed then it's much harder for it to absorb and use the nutrients it needs to keep you healthy.

Next time you look at a hamburger, bunch of fries or sugar-coated doughnut, go and put some orange juice in your car and see how well it works.

Why the AVOID list works

The AVOID list reduces your "chronic load". If you commit to it and stick to it you will quickly notice that you start to feel better and your vitality will increase. Focus on this feeling and your desire to eat the foods on the avoid list will reduce.

Are you saying I should never eat the AVOID items again?

Never say Never!

I had to avoid certain foods in order to rebuild myself. Now I eat some of the foods on the avoid list, but only in moderation. I simply don't feel like them anymore. I don't want sugar, bread or alcohol in the same way that I used to and that's the beauty of the rebuild. You re-educate your palate and you love feeling good instead of feeling unwell and out of control with your eating.

You stop using food as a crutch and turn it into your building block for health.

Now if I want chocolate I have good quality dark chocolate. I still treat it as an indulgence but where I used to wolf down half a box of cheap processed chocolate, now I have a couple of squares of "Green & Blacks Organic chocolate" and I feel really satisfied.

If you rebuild well, at some point in the future you'll become strong enough to tolerate (in moderation,) the foods that currently trigger you. Or you may find, you simply no longer desire them.

As I've said before, this is a journey. It's not about getting to the destination of good health and saying 'Great, now I can drink, smoke and eat crap all day'. The changes that will happen as part of your journey should make you look at nourishment in a different light.

When I started to feel better, I wanted more of it. When I started to feel great, I wanted to know what it would be like to feel fabulous. When I began to feel energised and fabulous on a regular basis, I said to myself, 'I am never going back there!'

I heard it said that the famous British supermodel Kate Moss once said,

'Nothing tastes as good as skinny feels.'

My version of that is,

'No junk tastes as good as healthy feels.'

What can I expect if I eat like this?

This will depend on your current state of health but you should feel more energised, less tired and more mentally alert. You may experience some detox symptoms when you remove certain foods or beverages from your diet, so make sure you always have your substitutes from the ADD column close to hand and try and keep yourself satiated. It's not about starving yourself. If you're not hungry you will be far less likely to succumb to snacks.

Should I check with my doctor?

If you are worried, of course, but before you do, read through again. Is there anything dangerous or difficult in this plan? I certainly hope not. This is a gentle rebuild that you can manage at your own pace.

What if I want to go full out?

This is totally up to you. Just remember that by reducing the stress on your system you will create release and this MUST be managed. If you've already tried any form of detox and given up because you felt dreadful then it's because the cleansing and releasing process wasn't being managed.

In the next section, I'll give you the tools and techniques to support yourself properly through a detox.

When can I have the AVOID foods again?

As a general rule, once you feel well and have done so for 3–6 months you may be able to cope with foods from the AVOID list, in moderation.

I stuck with the AVOID list for two years because that's what I needed. You will decide what's right for you and when you do, re-introduce items from the avoid list one food at a time. Notice how it makes you feel and only consume it in moderation.

The point of a rebuild is not to get better and then slip back into your unhealthy habits. Your goal is to create a stronger, healthier body that will endure. You want lasting vitality, not a relapse. I still largely avoid processed sugar, wheat and caffeine. They just don't agree with me and I like the leaner, energised person I am without them.

Be guided by how food makes you FEEL rather than what you think you want.

Cravings, Stress Eating and Dieting

How do I manage cravings?

Be proactive! A good protein breakfast goes a long way to stabilising your blood sugar. Protein at lunch and healthy snacks keep it stable throughout the day, and if you're well rested and taking exercise, those cravings should have a much harder time getting to you.

That said – it happens! So make sure you have a distraction plan ready.

Here are my top distractions to take your mind off cravings:

1. *Go out for a short walk – get away from the distraction and switch your senses on to what's around you. Surround yourself in nature if possible and do some deep breathing, stretches or gentle exercise.*

2. *Drink water – you may well be thirsty rather than hungry.*

3. *Find a substitute – learn to love something else instead and try and make it protein based as this will help stabilise your blood sugar.*

4. *Watch something funny – seriously, you won't believe how well this works. Get on YouTube and watch ten minutes of funny videos and laugh your heart out. You'll feel better and far less likely to want whatever it was. In fact, do this every day regardless. Laughter is always the best medicine.* ☺

Is your craving really a "Love Low"?

If you notice regular and repeated cravings, take a minute to go deeper. What's the emotion behind the craving?

Is it a sugar low or are you trying to replace a lack of love somewhere in your life with chocolate, a burger or coke?

Is the source of your "Love Low" actually YOU?

Here's an easy way to answer that – if you were totally happy, healthy, loved and engaged in fulfilling work, would you be reaching for that chocolate/burger/fries?

In my "Love Low" moments, I'd hunt down chocolate or brownies. Revelling in the sweetness – trying to replace what wasn't sweet in my life. For a brief moment, it felt like heaven and then within minutes it felt like hell. I'd be so dizzy and nauseous, I'd have to lie down on the floor.

When I gave up sugar for two years, it was as though a cloud lifted. My energy felt stronger and more consistent. I loved the way I felt so much I started to love myself for giving it up. This is a hugely important part of the healing process. I used to love sweets and cakes, but I LOVE the way I feel without them more.

.Just as you can be driven by your discontent with your current health so you can also be pulled by your longing for the health and vitality you want. USE THIS!

What about stress eating?

Eating because you're stressed isn't about food, but it happens because in an agitated or emotional state your brain produces a hormone called Ghrelin. Ghrelin makes food that's high in fat and calories seem very exciting and appealing.

In part, this dates back to our hunter-gatherer days when stress meant we were being chased by a wild animal… rather than our WIFI going down!

If you feel yourself getting stressed, walk away from the biscuit tin, drink a glass of water and spend five minutes of quiet time trying to figure out what the problem really is and how important it really is. The truth is unless you're about to die then you probably don't need that chocolate bar and it's unlikely to make the source of your stress go away.

If your job stresses you out, figure out what work you could do instead that would make you happy. If your relationship stresses you out, talk about it, get help, work through it. If friends stress you out, find someone else to hang out with. If money stresses you out, do the mindset work around it.

Am I over-simplifying? HELL YES! But here's my point – everything in life is a choice. Choose what makes you truly happy and healthy, repeatedly, and your life will change for the better. It's always an inside job.

Should I call this a diet?

No.

Diets are about willpower and willpower won't win against your biochemistry.

This is about a way of life. It's about re-balancing your biochemistry and becoming a more intuitive and mindful eater. As you become more conscious of the signals from your body you'll learn to eat when you're hungry, rather than when you're tired, bored or thirsty. You'll sit down and make time for food instead of shoving food in your mouth on the run, or grazing on snacks.

If you listen to when you're full, you'll stop eating. If you learn what makes you feel good long term, rather than seeking out a quick sugar, fat and salt hit, you will set yourself up for great health.

Obsessing about what you can't have from the AVOID list, only makes you want it more and your willpower's simply not strong enough to resist what your mind tells it you really, really want.

Research shows that people who diet usually regain the weight they lost within five years so remove the word diet from your vocabulary and get on with your rebuild.

Try this exercise if you're a meat eater. Notice what happens when you eat a great piece of steak. You feel full. The protein and fat in the meat leave you satiated. You might be able to eat six bagels but I guarantee you will stop long before you eat six steaks because the reaction in your body is different.

Don't compete with your biochemistry, aim for balance in your meals to create balance in your body.

Step Away from the Sugar

In 2007, Dr Mercola quoted a study that showed refined sugar to be more addictive than cocaine. This is something we're not often told considering how much sugar is added to everyday products.

You may think of sugar as the grainy white stuff that makes things taste good, but to your body, sugar is an immune suppressant and carbohydrate. If you don't burn carbohydrates your body lays them down to fat.

Here's what happens if you eat lots of sugar and processed foods:

1. *Your body has to make lots of insulin to try and normalise your blood sugar. But insulin is a fat storage hormone. With so much insulin swilling around the body, the cells eventually become insulin resistant. Now all the extra insulin floating around can't get into the cells so it goes to fat storage and typically accumulates around the waist.*

2. *Leptin is an appetite suppressing hormone. It literally stops you feeling hungry, but too much insulin blocks leptin, so your body actually thinks it's hungry, and you eat more! The body can't cope and gradually you become leptin resistant.*

Notice my word choice here. Gradually. This is not a foregone conclusion. You always have a choice. Just don't take too long to make it.

If you're female let me give you more motivation – Dr Mark Hyman cites insulin resistance as THE cause of ageing.

But surely as long as I burn it off I can have sugar?

Sorry, all calories are not created equal and the input vs output argument just doesn't hold up. It' not about calories, it's about how your body metabolises calories. So 100 calories of kale have a totally different effect to 100 calories of cake. Remember I said for every input, there's an effect? Did you know that you actually have to walk

4.5miles to burn off ONE 20oz can of soda? (And don't get me started on the other biological effects!)

But I love / need SUGAR!

No you don't. You love and need the way it makes you feel.

Throughout my childhood, and I suspect, nearly everyone's, sugar was used as a reward. If I did something good I got a sweet or a lollipop. If there was a celebration, a cake would be made. If I needed cheering up, a chocolate bar would do the trick.

It's no one's fault. It's just the way it was.

If like me, you've been programmed from childhood to associate sweet with pleasure and reward, now's the time to begin your re-education. See it as a wonderful experiment where you discover other things that can make you feel the same way.

Here are some of my suggestions:

1. *A few moments gazing at nature, appreciating your favourite picture or scene.*
2. *YouTube! Choose something funny or motivational.*
3. *A quick check of how far you've come. Even if that means giving yourself a pat on the back for surviving this far!*
4. *Five minutes focussing on the vision for your life that you'll create in section 7.*
5. *Love. Pure and simple. Focus on something or someone you love deeply for 3–5 minutes. Allow that feeling flood your body. Now try directing a little of that love at yourself.* ☺

Use these and come up with your own, including new healthy reward foods. As time goes on, it will get easier to find that sweetness inside yourself rather than on the shelf. ☺

How to Re-Programme Your Palate

When I started my rebuild, I gave up sugar, wheat, caffeine, alcohol and milk for two years. Yep, that's how bad I felt! Today for some people this might seem pretty average but back in 2001, I can guarantee you it was considered extreme!

My diet changed overnight as a lot of what I had eaten before was now off limits. I had to rethink my shopping and cooking but I stuck to simple meals, lots of alkalising vegetables and good quality meat and I noticed the difference right away. My fatigue eased and I noticed my energy levels increasing.

I started a Pilates class and although I cheated mercilessly for several months, very soon I was keeping up with the rest of the class. My body began to feel stronger. I didn't feel light headed all the time. It was as if my brain fog lifted.

Note here that I didn't add all the things in my recommended "ADD" section at first. I didn't know about them yet. At this point, I was just beginning my journey and it was clear to me that changing my fuel was changing my life. I stopped wanting anything that would make me feel bad. For the first time, I was really listening to my body.

As I discovered the foods in my "ADD" list, I incorporated them into my eating habits. I experimented and adapted over a period of years and I grew stronger as a result. Within two years of starting my rebuild, I could do a gentle dance class. After four years, I trained as a dance teacher and started teaching. After five years, I started playing netball. These were things I'd given up hope of EVER doing again.

Within seven years, I was playing full intensity, league level netball. Initially, each one-hour match was like a marathon for me but by then I trusted that, if I provided the right fuel, my body could do it. There were nights when I walked off jittery and light headed but I managed it with nourishment and the techniques in section 4.

I re-programmed my palate for health and I got vitality beyond belief. By year eight, I was playing netball, full out, with no jitters. I was also enjoying high energy dance classes, walking my dogs every day and most importantly, having the energy to be the mum I wanted to be.

It felt like a miracle. It was the result of a rebuild.

So Jacqueline, what do you eat?

On an average day, it tends to look like this:

Breakfast

Nettle tea or linseed tea and a couple of drops of Lugols (see below for information). Food choices range from:

Leftover meat and veg from night before.

Oat bran porridge made with almond milk, hemp powder, ground seed mix (This is what I give my kids and sweeten it slightly with pure maple syrup).

Eggs on rye toast.

Organic high fat yoghurt with some coconut oil added, protein powder and berries

Snack

Nuts, fruit, rice cakes, oatcakes, almond butter.

Lunch

Summer – salad with hummus, ground seed sprinkles, and meat or fish. Dried fruit or dark chocolate.

Winter – soup with rice noodles and seaweed strips + rye toast with a form of protein. Snack – Oatcakes, maybe with cheese, or almond butter. Linseed tea.

Dinner

Protein and vegetables and if I need something really stodgy a fish risotto with rice that has been cooked for at least an hour with more and more water added.

This is my long-term maintenance plan. I don't think of it as a diet and for the record, my weight hasn't fluctuated by more than 2kgs since I started eating this way fourteen years ago.

What's Lugols?

A solution of elemental iodine and potassium iodide in water, named after the French physician J.G.A. Lugol.

Here's a government quote on the importance of iodine.

> *'Iodine is a mineral found in some foods. The body needs iodine to make thyroid hormones. These hormones control the body's metabolism and many other important functions. The body also needs thyroid hormones for proper bone and brain development during pregnancy and infancy.'*

I learnt through my studies about the transformative nature of iodine and how deficiency results in ill health and supplementation benefits most conditions. For me, Iodine was transformative.

For more information on iodine, try the book *Iodine, Why You Need It, Why You Can't Live Without It* by Dr Brownstein.

Food Trends

There's always something new I'm told I should be eating

Food trends of recent years are all heading in the right direction, towards health, but if you find them overwhelming just stick with the ADD and AVOID list for now.

Juicing

Juicing is not healthier than eating whole fruits and vegetables but for some people it's easier. Juices can be very cleansing and nutritious but do try and use juices with the pulp intact, or add some of the pulp back into the juice to get the fibre, and always make sure your juice is heavily weighted towards vegetables to avoid a sugar rush.

I'm a huge fan of beetroot juice, which is a rich source of nitrates that help the body use oxygen more efficiently, especially after exercise.

Souping

Souping means having soup at every meal, usually fortified with superfoods to ensure a complete meal is achieved. If you have trouble digesting or would like to go through a cleansing period then souping can be a very warm and comforting way to do this.

Raw

The definition of raw food is uncooked, unprocessed and mostly organic food. However, if this conjures up images of cold, lank salad then think again. Raw food can be warmed to 118 degrees and the sensation of heat is usually added through spices. The science behind raw food says that the vitamins and mineral are better preserved when they are not heat treated, so raw food provides more nutrients to the body.

A good way to experiment with this concept is to add a bit of raw food to each meal or try one raw meal a day. Going raw will definitely create lots of release so try it at your pace and support the release with the Techniques in section 5.

Fermented food

Fermented foods contain beneficial bacteria which boosts our bowel health, considered by experts to be the seat of our immunity. Traditionally, we ate more fermented foods than we do now and sadly, a preference for sweet has de-popularised the slightly sour taste of fermented foods, but these foods have a very beneficial part to play in rebuilding and maintaining our health. Try adding some Kombucha or Sauerkraut to your diet, or check out the variety of Kefir drinks increasingly available in health food stores.

Gluten-free

If you experience gluten sensitivity then it is definitely worth having a gluten-free period. It's much easier than you think.

There are numerous gluten-free products available, but a word of caution. Check the label and try to find alternatives without lots of flavours, thickeners and sugars added. Sometimes "Gluten-free" on a label really means "but full of other stuff". My rule is, if there are lots of ingredients your granny wouldn't recognise then the chances are, neither will your body.

Encountering Resistance!

I don't have time for a complicated eating plan

Neither did I. That's why the ADD / AVOID list is designed to be very simple. The goal is to make nutrition work for you and leave you satiated, energised and brighter. The moment it becomes a chore, make a change, vary it.

Make soups and meals on the weekend and use throughout the week. Use healthy treats and don't do deprivation, this isn't about punishing yourself. Learn to enjoy food, savour tastes and flavours rather than going for quantity.

Re-programme your genes for health, survival and longevity.

Don't you ever cheat, Jacqueline?

Sure. My body is strong enough now that if I indulge in something on the AVOID list, my world doesn't fall apart. I can eat wheat products but they soon leave me feeling bloated, constipated and sluggish. It quickly reminds me why I prefer to avoid them.

What you need to know

This is not about never eating the foods on the AVOID list again. This is about rebuilding yourself to be strong enough to deal with them occasionally. There are always instances when we have to say 'What the hell'. We're human.

How we manage the result is the key. If I eat something that creates constipation, dehydration or stress by any other name. I manage it using the techniques in section 3.

What's next?

Now you've completed your fuel assessment and have nutritional guidelines to follow. You can begin to un-tease the tight knot of ill health and to do this you'll need support. In section 4, I'll show you how to set this up.

Journal Space

SECTION 4

SETTING UP YOUR SUPPORT

Journeys are easier with a friend and let's face it, we all need some backup. ☺

For much of my rebuild, I felt very isolated and alone. Apart from health practitioners, I knew no one who could relate to my situation or understand the journey I was going through. If you're experiencing something similar, then know right now, you have found your tribe. ☺

It's not easy being the person who doesn't drink alcohol, eat cake, indulge in a sugary dessert, medicate themselves at any opportunity and generally anaesthetise themselves through life. It can make other people feel uncomfortable. Often it brings up issues for them that they don't know how to face, so they back away or try and tear you down.

If you've ever been cajoled into "just one…" whatever, only to feel terrible later, you'll know what this is like.

Facing a rebuild alone can be a long, hard road. It's why people don't attempt it, or start but soon give up. It's why I wrote this book.

During part of my rebuild, I was an expat' living abroad, the community was very transient. People moved in and out, and I was constantly meeting new faces and turning down drinks and the foods that triggered me. I was quickly labelled a health freak and lost count of the number of times people asked me if I was a vegetarian! One well-meaning "friend" even remarked to his wife as she was pouring the wine at dinner, 'Don't waste it on Jacqueline, she won't drink it.'

He was right, but it still hurt.

Sometimes it's easier to let someone fill your glass and simply put it down somewhere later and never return to it. I've spent many parties with a tall glass of sparkling water, ice and lemon, passing it off as a gin and tonic.

Do what works for you and understand that constantly challenging people who make assumptions about you is a weary business. It's their stuff not yours and it's draining your energy, so let it go.

I always wondered what it would be like to have my husband stand up for me at a social gathering. I imagined being challenged for not drinking, or called out for being a party pooper. As the challenger tried to cajole me into alcohol or openly called me boring, my husband would casually step in and wax lyrical on how great I looked and how strong and healthy I was and, by the way, how much fun I was, even without alcohol!

It never happened but here's the learning – in the end I started to do this for myself and that was part of the journey. I now have no problem taking a stand for anything I believe in, or supporting others when I see they need it.

In writing this book, I thought about what I needed, what I would have loved and what I wanted to set up to help you. Read on to discover the steps you can take to support yourself now.

7 Steps to Solid Support

1. Find Your Tribe

Be open to meeting like-minded people, whether in person or online. Expect them to become part of your life. Make time for them and before they show up, imagine what it will feel like to be part of a like-minded community, or to have a friend who feels the same way and is perhaps interested in coming on this journey with you.

Decide that you will make an effort to talk to people if they come into your life. Be open to meeting members of your tribe online.

Bear in mind that as with any relationship, it's not about dumping your stuff on someone else and expecting them to fix it. Nor is it an opportunity to complain and have someone say "Poor you" as this only holds you in your ill health. It's about finding people who are positively taking charge of their health and making a commitment to join them, to support them and in so doing, to support yourself.

2. Instead of a Book Club, Start a Cook Club

As one of my favourite authors, Jean Houston, says,

> *'There is nothing the human imagination working in community cannot accomplish.'*

Find local friends within the Rebuild community and take it in turns to cook for each other once a week, once a month or whatever works. Never underestimate the power of community to motivate and support each other. Enjoy the gift of discovering new healthy recipes together. Invest in healthy cookbooks that make you want to eat well.

It doesn't need to be expensive. You can join a library or buy cookbooks as a group and share them. You can pair up and cook with a friend, or you can cook as a group and make enough for two or three meals for everyone. Working together in this way is supporting each other and it's incredibly nurturing and keeps the focus on creating health, rather than illness.

3. Getting support from a partner

Your partner is the person who probably cares most about you and you may find them totally supportive or you may meet unexpected resistance. In either case, don't let them pressure you into making choices that leave you uneasy.

This is your body and your journey.

Take responsibility for yourself, decide the best course of action and don't justify your choices more than that. Battling against someone else's ideology is draining and your energy is needed to rebuild. If you have people who constantly challenge you, make it clear, once, that you're taking a stand for your health. If that's bringing up THEIR health stuff, it's something they need to deal with, not you.

Discuss your choices once but don't keep repeating yourself. If they can't get on board, give yourself some distance, and if you can't create distance (maybe you're married to them) tell them kindly and lovingly that this what you're doing and you'd love their support but if they can't give it, you'll take their silence instead.

In the early days of my rebuild, I didn't share my learning with my husband or tell him how I was applying it. He couldn't get his head around what had happened. It was his way of coping. As my health improved, he became more tolerant and interested as he could see something was changing. It's a process. If you meet resistance, ask for patience and as you get stronger and healthier, expect their interest and understanding to materialise.

4. How to get buy in if you have kids

If you change the menu at home you'll probably get a reaction!

Remember the best gift you can give your kids is good health. It might not be realistic to expect them to embrace the ADD / AVOID list immediately but you can begin to make changes. Slowly move away from rewarding them with candy as a treat or having sugary cereals and processed foods in the house.

This removes temptation for you and starts to broaden their palate. Don't expect their taste buds to change overnight, but over time they will become more receptive. Keep offering it every now and then. Be the best role model and let them watch the change in you.

My kids now eat all manner of things they turned their noses up at initially. Over a period of time, I reinforced the message of health and they began to understand why.

ADD foods were good and made them stronger and healthier. After a while, they spontaneously began to make smarter choices around food. Do they still have chocolate and junk? Yes, every now and then but the difference is, they know what they're doing and they don't do it often.

It's not your job to heal someone else, but you can educate and support them into making great choices.

5. How to get support from a close friend

A true friend will love and support you in your quest for health, but expect it to bring up stuff for them! Friendship is a journey as much as health is, and if you've been unwell for a while, years maybe, then they may be so afraid of losing you that they can't get past that fear.

Conversely, if they dump you because you'll no longer engage in the drinking, binge eating or some other toxic activity then now's the time to find better friends! Understand that as you move forward in this journey there will be parts of your old life that you need to cut away from, in order to become the person you want to be.

Rebuilding is a growth process and, as in nature, there is a natural shedding that occurs. Don't cling on to anything too tightly. If it's meant to be part of the new you, it will be. If it's not, let it go lovingly. New people will come to fill any void. Stay open and receptive. It will happen.

6. Consider the alternative

If you're not getting the answers or support you need from conventional medicine then it's time to look elsewhere. Over the course of my rebuild, I spent thousands on alternative practitioners, books and education that helped me understand what had happened to my health.

I don't regret a penny of it. ☺ In fact, I love how my health and my life has transformed as a result, but luckily, you don't need to spend thousands – most of what I learnt is in this book and today so much information is also available online.

Alternative health was an endless source of support and inspiration for me. As I hope you will begin to see, it's often the simplest things that have the biggest impact. The very action of becoming interested and taking responsibility creates hope.

In section 10, you will find a list of all the alternative health practices I tried and the books I loved. Do some research and try an alternative approach or the alternative therapist that instinctively feels right for you. No one therapy or practitioner is likely to cure you, but they are excellent stepping stones to take you to the next level of health as you rebuild.

7. How to support yourself

Seems obvious doesn't it, but all too often we are sabotaging our best efforts with our thoughts and actions. Give yourself the space to heal.

If you're tempted by what someone's eating, remind yourself how it will make you feel (and then walk away quickly!). If you're tempted by toxic situations, people or substances, distract yourself with something that you know makes you feel good and creates health.

Always have your end game in mind – if it doesn't move you towards great health, move away from IT!

Get organised. If foods on the AVOID list are your biggest temptation then clear them from your cupboards, shop for and plan meals in advance. Use the weekends to try new recipes or make larger dishes to see you through the start of the week.

If you hear yourself saying 'I really can't go without…' write down how that food makes you feel and why you're not getting that in your life. What action can you take to bring it into your life?

If you can't remember what great health felt or looked like, remind yourself. Go through some old photos or memorabilia of how you used to feel, or find images that represent that for you. Put them somewhere where you'll see them every day. Always keep it positive by focussing on what you WANT rather than want you no longer want.

Many people use vision boards as part of this practice. Creating a clear mental picture or your "vision" is very useful in your rebuild and we will go through this process in section 7.

Take a stand for your health, repeatedly and consistently. Make changes. Take action and remind yourself that NOTHING is more important than you being the healthiest version of yourself, physically, mentally, emotionally and spiritually.

Make a choice to recognise and believe in your potential to heal on a daily basis.

I'm feeling overwhelmed!!!

That's your ego talking. ☺

By trying to keep you in a state of confusion, it knows you will remain stuck where you are. So if what we've covered so far feels like a lot to digest then simply pick one thing you'll start this week and do it.

Consistent, repetitive action is key.

Add in other elements of the programme, week by week. Don't overload yourself otherwise it's tempting to give up and go back to the same old patterns. Don't under-load yourself as the lack of change could prove demotivating.

Remember to make these changes gradually and according to your energy levels. It's not about making health happen, it's about making health welcome. You create the conditions for health and health naturally follows.

Now let's move on to section 5 and "My 3 Golden Rules of Rebuilding".

Journal Space

SECTION 5

MY 3 GOLDEN RULES OF REBUILDING

If you really want this Rebuild to a) work and b) last, then there are three simple but golden rules to follow.

1. Release

Here we focus on the physical side of your rebuild and the need to cleanse. I'll talk you through old-fashioned but highly effective techniques to detox and support yourself physically through illness and into long-term wellbeing. These are simple tools and life skills that will help you through a health crisis. Support yourself through a detox, heal at your pace and use them on an ongoing basis to maintain optimal health. If you want results, you'll love this.

2. Rest and Relaxation

Differentiating between pretend and proper R&R and how to incorporate it into your life.

3. Remember

The one crazy but important thing you MUST do!

Let's dive in!

Rule Number 1 – Release

Now that you know how to reduce the stress on your body and nourish yourself, you will begin to see movement as your body finds the energy to detoxify. When your body starts this process of release, it's important to support it, to ensure toxins leave the body.

Releasing toxins from your body is a two-part process.

a. *Release through movement – this requires stimulation of your lymphatic system. Your lymph runs alongside your blood vessels and as the blood pumps, the toxins are deposited from the blood into the lymph and out of the body. So the first way to facilitate release is quite simply, to move.*

b. *Release through techniques – what we might call old-fashioned methods of encouraging and supporting the body to offload toxicity.*

Release Through Movement

Whether it's gentle or vigorous, physical activity plays a huge role in your rebuild and I would go as far as to say that if you're not actively moving, you're actively contributing to your toxification. When you exercise you effectively "heat" the body. This stimulates the body to push toxins to the skin, from where they can be sweated out and washed away.

From a gentle walk or yoga class to something more energetic with an instructor, do what feels right for your energy level and most importantly, do what feels good.

If you feel unwell then don't make exercise something that adds to your stress. Choose something pleasurable, something that makes you smile. Get creative.

Did you know this?

'Just half an hour of walking every day can protect against a range of chronic diseases and help prevent premature death. It also slows the progression of Alzheimer's and reduces arthritic pain.'*

Walking outside in the sunshine is an added bonus. It is no coincidence that I noticed a marked improvement in my health when I moved to South Africa. My vitamin D levels soared and I felt stronger. I'm not suggesting everyone move to the southern hemisphere, but when the sun shines, get out in it for ten minutes and absorb some rays without sunscreen. If you're really fair sit in the shade but take off your glasses and let the bright sunshine flood in.

Did you know this?

Researchers at the Dana-Farber Cancer Institute found that people with high levels of vitamin D (the sunshine vitamin) are more likely to survive cancer for longer.**

But I just don't have the energy to exercise

If you are really unwell I know exercise can seem impossible. It felt that way for me, so I started with Pilates because most of the class was spent lying down and it was very easy to cheat! I could fake most of the small concentrated movements and when I'd had enough I could lie and do nothing while the teacher was looking the other way.

The important thing was that I was at the class. I made a commitment to getting stronger, and gradually, I found that I didn't need to cheat. I stopped faking and after several months, through just two classes a week I was noticeably stronger, and I had the beginnings of a six-pack!

From Pilates, I progressed to a gentle dance class. Again it was something that I could do at a very low level and there was something about the music that, in itself, was healing.

---

* Source: www.telegraph.co.uk
** Source WDDTY April 2015.

The message is this – Do the exercise that appeals to you. Aim for movement each day and make it a pleasure. ☺

I'm too unwell to get out of bed

Then start in bed. Google the videos on YouTube with exercises and stretches for those confined to their beds. You are not alone.

You can also set aside time each day to imagine yourself exercising. Don't knock it. Olympic athletes use this tool frequently to visualise themselves performing and winning at their chosen event. You don't need to imagine you're Usain Bolt but choose your favourite sport and, in your mind's eye, see yourself doing it.

Close your eyes and sense the strength in your muscles as you move, easily and with grace. Feel the power in your body and see yourself smiling as you walk, jog, run or whatever you've chosen. Feel the steady rhythm of your strong heartbeat, the perspiration on your skin as sweat out toxins. Imagine how great it would feel to be exercising. This is something you can do every day until exercise becomes possible for you. Remember that if your mind can conceive it, your body can achieve it. Let yourself buy into your own potential.

If all you can do is open a window and do some deep breathing exercises, do it. Taking any form of action is the most important step. It shows your body you're on the starting block and you're ready to rebuild.

Now let's look at part b, Releasing Through Techniques.

Release Through Techniques

While it's important to facilitate the release of toxins from your cells, it's equally important to ensure the released toxicity can actually leave the body. I've met lots of people who have attempted a detox, whether nutritional or physical, only to quickly give up because the effects made them feel worse than before they started.

If you've tried a detox and suffered headaches, lethargy, aches or other side effects, it's likely you stimulated a release but were unable to complete the cycle by allowing complete removal. In simple terms, toxicity may have left your cells but ended up swilling around in your body, making you feel worse!

Using simple techniques enable this release from the body. Techniques create movement and can be used to target specific areas or blocks.

Imagine a large rubbish truck or dumpster, it's full of rubbish that needs to be taken away but it has run out of fuel. It can't move. The rubbish sits there and it's a nice warm day so it starts to decompose, decay and generally smell. It gets more and more toxic until finally, someone fills up the fuel tank and off the truck goes to be emptied.

In this example, the truck needed a little extra support, so that it could offload. The equivalent support you can use for your body are techniques.

What are techniques?

Quite possibly your new best friend! ☺

The techniques I am going to recommend are unashamedly old-fashioned. They are the kind of excellent support that was offered to patients in days gone by, now sadly forgotten.

Today, we tend to medicate symptoms away rather than releasing the toxicity that creates the symptom. This is nothing short of a tragedy as techniques are cheap, effective and work with the body instead of against it. If I had been taught them early on in my illness, I would have been far better equipped to deal with my health crisis!

Here's what you need to know:

Illness and disease are the result of stagnation in the body. Stagnation is the loss of the body's ability to cleanse.

Techniques create freedom and movement in an effort to restore balance and wellness.

Techniques vary from culture to culture and you may have some of your own to add to your toolbox.

Using techniques

When you use a technique, do so sympathetically. Your goal is to create a manageable amount of release. This process is about eliminating toxicity at a rate that suits your condition, so don't be afraid to start slowly and build up.

Each time you release a little more toxicity you can re-evaluate your state of health and plan the next technique accordingly. It's a process of peeling back the layers of illness to return to gradual and sustainable health.

Try the techniques that resonate with you and don't dismiss those that seem outlandish. I learnt about enemas years before I was mentally ready to try one and I paid a high-health price as a result. I was willing to suffer more than I was willing to try something that, at the time, seemed crazy. Now I wish I hadn't waited so long!

When the sh*t hits the fan, in your worst state of illness, you may feel willing to try anything. This is a good sign. It means you're highly teachable and receptive – use this. Stay open to what might help you.

Types of Techniques

Skin Brushing

Your skin is your largest organ of elimination and brushing it targets your lymph system and encourages release so that less toxicity passes through your internal organs. It's a similar release to exercise and gentle sweating and, if you can't, or aren't well enough to exercise, then skin brushing is a great way to create gentle movement.

What do I need to know?

This can stimulate release from your bowels, so make sure you're able to go to the toilet and release. If you're constipated, address that using diet and hydration before trying this.

Only skin brush on dry skin. Never brush on varicose veins or eczema.

How often should I skin brush?

You can safely use this technique once a day, on a daily basis.

What do I need?

A long-handled, fairly stiff brush. The long handle makes it easier to reach your back. Keep this brush just for skin brushing and always brush on dry skin with a dry brush. A wet brush will not be as effective.

How do I do it?

Follow these written instructions or go the resources page of www.rebuildyourhealthreclaimyourlife.com to watch a video.

1. *Use gentle but brisk strokes working from the top of the right foot up the right leg, front and back.*
2. *Repeat on the left leg, working up from the top of the left foot.*

3. *Brush the front torso up towards the heart. Do the same on the back torso.*

4. *Start at the right hand and brush up your right arm, front and back, all the way to the shoulder.*

5. *Repeat on the left arm, starting at the left hand.*

6. *Brush down from the back of your neck to the heart.*

7. *Gently brush from the front of your neck down towards the heart.*

How will I feel?

A bit like you've done some gentle exercise. Refreshed, alert and slightly tingly to really maximise the effect of skin brushing it's a good idea to follow it with a hot and cold shower.

Hot and cold showering

This is a great way to follow skin brushing as the hot and cold showering continues to target the circulatory and lymphatic systems. Under the hot shower the blood will move to the surface of the skin, and under the cold shower the blood moves back inwards to keep the vital organs warm and balance the internal temperature. This movement back and forth encourages release of toxins.

What do I need to know?

If you are asthmatic, or have a heart condition, high blood pressure or are pregnant, start at a warm temperature and adjust to cool. You can build the temperature differential as you feel comfortable to avoid a sudden shock to the chest area.

How often should I do it?

Once a day is great. First thing in the morning is usually the best time as it creates movement after a deep sleep, but this technique can be practised at any time of day.

What do I need?

A normal shower with good temperature control.

How do I do it?

Start with your shower at a normal temperature and stand for a few minutes underneath.

Turn the temperature down until it is comfortably cool for you. Stay at that temperature for about thirty seconds, until the body feels cold, or as cool as is tolerable.

Turn the temperature to hot, or as warm as is comfortable and stand under for thirty seconds or until the body feels hot, or as warm as is tolerable.

Repeat this process three times. Finish on a cold or cool setting.

As you get used to this technique, you can increase the temperature differentials to suit you.

How will I feel?

Refreshed, alert and awake. This is a great morning kickstart if you can be sluggish.

Epsom salts bath

This is a personal favourite as it is so easy and very relaxing and uses the skin as a route of elimination. Epsom salts are made up of magnesium sulphate, which draws toxicity towards itself. So if you are in a bath of Epsom salts the salts draw toxicity in your body out through the skin into the bath water.

The warmth of the bath water encourages your cells to eliminate toxicity and send it to the skin's surface where it can be washed away. The combination of the heat of the bath and the action of the Epsom salts stimulate a lot of movement within the body, but this is a very relaxing process.

What do I need to know?

Avoid if you are at risk of haemorrhaging or if you have high blood pressure or are pregnant. This technique is also best avoided while menstruating as the body is already in a state of elimination.

Do not add anything else to the bathwater. Bath bubbles, oils etc. should be avoided so as to concentrate the effect of the salts.

This is an excellent technique to use if you have sore muscles, aches and pains. For the onset of a sore throat or swollen glands in the neck, this is my technique of choice and can help nip a cold in the bud. If you are unable to get into a bath or you don't have one, you can also do an Epsom salts footbath for a soothing alternative.

How often should I do it?

Try one bath to start and then work up to two or three times a week for three weeks and then take a break for a week. Always do this technique at night as this is when the body uses magnesium to cleanse the cells. It also has a very relaxing effect and is perfect before bed to encourage a good night's sleep.

What do I need?

A bathtub.

Up to 1kg of Epsom salts. (Available online. I buy from eBay in a 25kg bag as it's cheaper.)

How do I do it?

Run a warm to hot bath, pour 1kg of Epsom salts into it and stir to dissolve. Lie in the bath for 20 minutes, or work up to 20 minutes as it feels comfortable for you. If the bath is still warm you can add cold water to cool the body down, or take a cool shower. Otherwise, get out and dry as normal.

How will I feel?

Relaxed, tired and possibly a little weak. I recommend going to bed afterwards to enjoy a good night's sleep after which you should feel very refreshed and clearheaded.

Epsom salts footbath

If you do not have a bath, or cannot get into a bath, this is a relaxing alternative using the same Epsom salts as above to draw out toxicity.

What do I need to know?

An Epsom salts footbath is a perfect starting point when you want to create movement slowly within the body as the effects are very mild.

How often should I do it?

Up to five times a week or as you feel it is necessary. Before bed is the optimal time for this technique due to the relaxation and elimination it stimulates.

What do I need?

A footbath or washing up size bowl. 4 tablespoons of Epsom salts. A blanket and towel.

How do I do it?

Put the Epsom salts into the footbath and add hot water, or as warm as you can stand and stir to dissolve. Place the towel next to the footbath. Sit comfortably and place your feet in the footbath. If comfortable, cover yourself with a blanket to encourage the body to heat up and eliminate toxins. Keep your feet in the footbath for 20 minutes if possible. Remove your feet and dry them off.

How will I feel?

Relaxed, possibly tired, warm.

Cold foot wrap

This technique is particularly useful if you have a persistent headache as it draws blood away from the head and down to the feet to warm them and maintain the temperature balance within the body.

What do I need to know?

This is a very gentle technique, safe for most people.

How often should I do it?

As required, up to once a day.

What do I need?

One pair of cotton socks. One pair of woollen socks or a warm blanket.

How do I do it?

Soak the cotton socks in cold water, rinse and put them in the freezer for 10 minutes then remove from the freezer and put them on your feet.

Put the woollen socks on your feet or wrap a blanket around your feet and rest for 20mins.

Sitz bath

The effects of a sitz bath are similar to those of hot and cold showering, in that it creates movement within the circulatory and lymphatic systems and stimulates release from the bowel. It's also excellent for targeting the pelvic area and can be very helpful where there is muscular weakness e.g. weak or prolapsed organs. Sitz baths are good for prostate, fertility, and bowel problems and also fallopian blockages.

What do I need to know?

Do not use this technique if you are at risk of haemorrhaging or if pregnant.

How often should I do it?

As required but no more than once per day.

What do I need?

A normal bath and a small tub, such as a baby bath. If you do not have a bath you can use two small tubs, or you can do a smaller version of this in a bidet.

How do I do it?

Fill the bath with about 5 inches of hot water. Fill the small tub with about 5 inches of cold water. Pulling your knees up towards you, sit in the bath of hot water for a few minutes and splash the hot water over your torso. Change baths and sit in the cold water for several minutes, splashing the cold water over your torso. Repeat this 3 times and always finish on cold. Dry yourself vigorously to continue creating movement.

How will I feel?

This technique creates movement so you may feel the need to relieve your bladder or bowels.

Enemas

If you have ever thought about a colonic then, in my experience, an enema is a gentler form of this type of cleansing. Enemas are an ancient healing technique that target all areas from the cell to the bowel. Water is introduced into the bowel to create movement within the colon and encourage the release of stored faeces and stimulate reflex points within the colon that are connected to the entire body.

What do I need to know?

Follow the ADD and AVOID plan for a week before you try an enema, to ensure a detox process has started. Don't try this when you're hungry, your blood sugar is low, or if you're pregnant.

How often should I do it?

An enema is a more intensive technique so I recommend trying a basic water enema to start. You may find you cannot hold onto the water for any amount of time and this is perfectly normal, so practice and allow yourself time to adjust. A weekly enema is a good start point, although if you wish to create greater movement, three days in a row is worth considering.

Bear in mind that there are many different types of enema that you can do and for a more comprehensive programme, I recommend seeking professional support.

What do I need?

An enema kit – essentially a gravity feed enema bag with a long tube attached and a nozzle. These can be bought online. A two-pint jug filled with body temperature water. If you don't have a suitable hook then use a simple coat hanger to hang the bag. A warm, private, comfortable space to recline and perform the enema. A waterproof sheet is recommended although I manage perfectly fine with towels. Cushions or a pillow. A small amount of Vaseline or lubricant.

How do I do it?

1. *Hang the enema bag on a hook or coat hanger about 1m above where you will lie.*

2. *Check the tap on the enema bag is closed and then pour 2 pints of body temperature clean (filtered if possible) water into the bag.*

3. *Allow a small amount of water to run through the tube and out the other end to release any air bubbles.*

4. *Lubricate your anal area then lie on your back on the towels, or if you prefer, on your side. Use the pillow to support your head.*

5. *Take the nozzle at the end of the enema bag tube and insert it gently into your anus, then open the tap and allow the water to flow gently into your bowel.*

6. *Try and hold onto the water for five minutes or longer. This water can be absorbed by the bowel and use to combat dehydration. If you experience*

discomfort you can massage your abdomen and try deep breathing exercises to relax. I appreciate it is an unusual sensation at first.

7. *When you have had enough or you can no longer hold onto the enema, move to the toilet to release the fluid.*

How will I feel?

If you are suffering from constipation you will feel immediate relief. A certain lightness is usually experienced and mental clarity can be another positive side effect. If you are dehydrated after a long haul flight, an enema can make you feel refreshed.

Allow yourself time to rest afterwards which is advisable if you feel light headed.

Colonics

Colonics are a powerful tool as they stimulate all the reflexes in the body. A colonic is like an internal massage, but different from an enema as the water is pushed up into the colon using a machine, so more release can be achieved. Approximately 15 litres of water passes through the colon using a special device that allows water to flow in and waste to flow out simultaneously.

The first 5 litres pass through the colon while you lie on your left side so that cleansing focusses on the descending colon. The remaining 10 litres are usually administered while you lie on your back so that the water can reach the far side of your colon.

If you are crossing your legs and groaning this might not be for you yet. I would get comfortable with an enema or two and then try a colonic. They are an amazing form of release and are particularly good if done during the spring when the liver naturally wants to detox.

What do I need to know?

As with an enema, follow the ADD and AVOID plan for a week first, to ensure the body is prepared so as not to overload the liver. This is definitely something to try with the support of a practitioner as he/she will have the correct equipment and can manage the release for you. Do not use colonics if you have a prolapsed organ in the pelvic area, haemorrhoids or if you are pregnant.

How often should I do it?

It really depends on your state of health. Most practitioners recommend an initial colonic followed by another a month later, but you may need more or less according to your illness or symptoms, so take professional advice.

Colonics are particularly useful if you are constipated, or want to accelerate your cleansing process.

What do I need?

Make an appointment with a colonics therapist as this requires specialist equipment.

How will I feel?

It's usual to feel a little tired and light headed after a colonic, although I have met many people who feel rejuvenated and energised. It really depends on you and the level of toxicity that you are able to release.

I've never heard of these techniques.

I understand and I appreciate that some of them may cause you to baulk. I know when a practitioner recommended an enema to me, I left very quickly and couldn't even contemplate it. I was in such a fearful state that I simply couldn't hear or process the support my practitioner knew would help me. Once I'd improved and was on the path of re-building myself, it no longer seemed as scary to contemplate techniques.

Two years later, when I got around to trying some water-based therapy, I realised she was right and kicked myself for waiting so long.

Whatever your reaction to techniques, don't stress out and don't rule anything out. This is a process and within it is some great information that you will come back to, and take action on, when the time is right for you. Techniques can be a very relaxing experience and certainly an empowering one as you are able to control the application of each technique and adjust them to your needs. Remember that disease is a stagnated picture and techniques create freedom and movement which, in my opinion, is what healing is all about.

Rule Number 2 – Real Rest and Relaxation

Let's talk about stress

I read some research recently that a full night's sleep (8 hours) lowers cortisol by 20%. Cortisol is a hormone that helps the body respond to stress. If you have consistently high cortisol levels it means that you are stressed and excess cortisol in the body causes hormone imbalance and mood swings – not what you need as part of a balanced rebuild!

When you experience stress, your body thinks it is under attack and it diverts vital energy from other functions, like your metabolism and your immune system, to deal with the threat. In effect, the cortisol shuts down your immune response so the vital processes of repair and rejuvenation can't take place.

The interesting thing is that your body does not differentiate between different types of stress. It just feels stressed. So whether you're preparing for an important presentation and your laptop dies or you're having a meltdown because you're late and there are three people in front of you at Starbucks, to your body it's all the same.

Stress creates a response in our body and this is okay if it's a quick burst, but how many people do you know who are constantly on the go? They make phone calls while at the gym or multi-tasking on their iPad, and do their accounts while watching TV.

In traditional Chinese medicine, unresolved or perpetual stress for a sustained period of 2 years, is enough to send the body into a dehydrated state. The cells cannot cleanse properly when the body is dehydrated and this is seen as the beginning of disease.

Are we conscious of this? Probably not. In the developed world, we have become nations that never stop. Our holidays are spent desperately trying to relax and simultaneously trying to cram in everything we don't have time for.

We're constantly trying to "have it all" and this creates stress and stress creates illness.

Imagine a huge plate full of cake, a beautiful assortment of all your favourites and some new ones you'd like to try. (If cake doesn't work for you, insert chocolate, cheese, or your favourite food.)

Now imagine trying to eat the whole lot in one sitting. By the end of "having it all", the chances are you'll feel pretty sick. In the same way, trying to have it all in life, can lead us to illness. It's not about doing things perfectly and it's certainly not about doing it all at once. It's about savouring each stage, each phase and learning what you need to learn, before you move on to the next. Give yourself permission to be patient.

Consider the frequency with which you say or hear someone else say, 'I'm stressed out!'

What can I do about stress?

Have you heard this expression?

> *'Don't sweat the small stuff… it's all small stuff.'*

I know it doesn't feel like that when it's your health, but it's a good place to start. Decide when it's really worth getting stressed about something. Hint: the answer is always not very often!

The "something" or the stimulus of your stress is not important. In every circumstance and situation, you actually get to choose how you will respond. You can choose stress, fear, panic or you can consciously choose peace and calm.

This doesn't happen overnight, but it's a practice worth starting now.

If today was the end of the world for everyone. If at midnight tonight planet Earth would be no more for any of us, what would really matter to you?

Focus on those things and you will feel your heart rate lower. It's not that you should stop trying to achieve. It's that you should take the pressure out of trying. How many things on your to-do list are really what you want versus what you think you want?

It took me years to learn that trying to over-control outcomes in life creates misery and actually blocks what we want. So next time you start to feel frantic about needing to have, or achieve something RIGHT NOW, take a few deep breaths and look around you. Release the need to control and allow calming energy to flow through you.

Trust your intuition. Ask for help from something greater than you. Fully appreciate where you are and what it's taken to get here. Absorb the learning, the development, the lessons, good and bad and give yourself a pat on the back for making it this far.

Re-assure yourself that your good will come to you in the right way at the right time. Hold this intention and keep taking steps towards health and being open to receiving. In this mindset, change is inevitable.

How to enjoy the moment

Don't be too quick to gloss over what you have.

Recognise the only person who decides how much happiness you have in ANY given moment is YOU.

I look back at times in my life when I had two happy, healthy children, a loving husband, a great house, money in the bank, a supportive family and yet I wasn't happy. I was too busy wanting the next thing.

What I learnt the hard way is the necessity of being in the present and finding happiness in right now, because right now is all that really matters. I love this little saying because it sums it up so neatly.

> *'Yesterday is history, tomorrow is a mystery but today is a gift. That's why it's called the present.'*

Next time you go into overwhelm or stress, turn your focus back to right now and what you actually need to do in this moment, then do that. Over time, you'll find this creates a sense of peace which allows you to flow with life more easily.

Try this simple but powerful exercise to re-think what you want.

Write a list of all the things you thought you wanted before you became ill. Material possessions, relationships, experiences, money, put it all down.

Now cross out the ones that no longer seem important or AS important and instead write what you'd like to create in your life that has real meaning for you. By the side of each, write WHY it has meaning for you. The WHY is the most important factor. It guides who you're here to be.

Taking Time Out

If your body has given you any kind of symptoms, it's asking for a time out. When the body forces us to stop, it means we really have gone too far. Your body cannot spend time repairing you if it never gets a break.

I fully understand how easy it is to medicate or suppress symptoms away. Ignorance is bliss and I certainly indulged. I thought I was invincible. I pushed on and told my body to get over it, but instead of getting better, I got worse.

The only way to heal is to take the time to heal. If you cannot relax, how can your cells? You know exactly what it's like to have a million things to do and then someone gives you another big job. You throw our hands up and say, 'That's it, I can't do it all!'

Your body is no different.

Where are you on the rest and relaxation scale?

Go through the "Taking Time Out" exercise below and answer honestly:

How much time do you have for yourself each day?

Of this time, how much is spent in a consciously relaxed or resting state?

When you are resting or relaxed, how do you feel?

How many hours sleep are you getting on average?

How do you feel when you wake in the morning?

Can you get through the day without feeling tired or needing a nap?

Don't underestimate the power of relaxation or calming activities and their effect on your health. It's no accident that people who meditate live longer.

I try to relax but...

I know, there's always something, right? Whether it's a physical issue, or a worrying thought that plays over and over in your mind.

Here are some simple suggestions that helped me learn to REALLY rest, relax and support myself during my rebuild.

Rest and Relaxation Guide

1. *Set aside time for yourself each day, even if it's only 15 minutes at first. Read, listen to music, meditate or gaze at a view that you love.*

   Did you know...

   When you look at beautiful scenery or listen to uplifting music it creates an anti-inflammatory response in your body? It's nature's drug and it's as powerful as if you were medicating yourself. Try it. Indulge yourself in a picture, a view or some music and give yourself permission to get lost in it for five minutes.

2. *Try a guided meditation or visualisation to take your mind off stress and focus it on what you want in your health and your life. Visit the resources page of my website to find free mediations and visualisation exercises.*

   Bear in mind that compared to a full night's sleep which lowers cortisol levels by 20%, twenty minutes of meditation lowers cortisol levels by 30%.

3. *Try simple stretching or yoga exercises*

   Often doing some simple stretches can focus the mind on the physical and turn down the mental chatter. Visit the resources page of my website to find a simple stretch routine:

4. *Write it down*

   If you feel stressed even when you are resting, take a pen and write down what's stressing you. Look a little deeper and see if it's really about the "thing" that is worrying you, or a pattern or fear that keeps repeating in your life.

Expressing it on paper helps you to witness the worry. From here you can write down the action you will take to resolve the issue or you can simply choose to release it for the time of your relaxation period.

How to Supercharge Your Sleep

Here are some simple steps to help maximise your body's healing time overnight.

- *Make sure you allow yourself time to wind down.*

- *Turn off screens and phones so your body gets the message that you're preparing for rest. Don't stimulate your mind with phone calls or check your emails and then expect your body to know you want to switch off into a deep sleep.*

- *Do some deep breathing techniques. Deep breathing stimulates your vagus nerve which encourages your body to produce hormones to calm your nervous system.*

- *As you lie in bed, before turning off the light, write a gratitude list. With a pen and paper make a simple list of all the things you are grateful for in your life. I understand if you feel like there's not a lot to be appreciative of right now, so start small. Anything from your loved ones, to the food you eat, the warm, safe, comfortable home you live in, or the water that comes out of your tap.*

If you find you need inspiration, take a moment to consider life in a starving African country or a war zone. Be grateful for you have instead. Gratitude puts your body in the right frame of mind for healing.

I never wake refreshed

If you wake in the morning, still feeling tired and have to drag yourself out of bed then you know the cellular cleansing process that should happen overnight has not taken place properly. Make sure you are well hydrated and try an Epsom salts bath for 3 consecutive nights.

I always wake up at 2am/3am/4am

If you wake regularly at the same time each night, check the traditional Chinese medicine "organs by time" chart below. It's an over-simplified explanation but it's helpful. See if there are times that regularly crop up for you then read the explanation alongside:

High times of energy passing through organs

11pm – 1am

Gallbladder related to: Anger, resentment and frustration

Action: Find someone you can talk to, to safely express your anger. On a physical level, help the body by avoiding hydrogenated fats and using good oils instead (hemp, flax, coconut).

1am – 3am

Liver related to: Anger, irritation and frustration

Action: Safely express your emotions. Write them down and then destroy if necessary, tell a friend, coach or counsellor or call a support line, but get it out, let it go and focus on all the good in your life instead.

3am – 5am

Lungs related to: Grief and depression

Action: Notice when you hear yourself sigh and do some deep breathing exercises to release tension. Try and get some fresh air every day and sleep with the window open a little at night if possible. If you feel sadness and grief, talk to a friend or counsellor, write a daily list of everything you are grateful for and practice the gratitude audio exercise on the resources page of the website.

5am – 7am

Large Intestine/bowel related to: Sluggish elimination of toxins. Difficulty letting something in life go. Often connected to the lungs.

Action: Avoid foods that make you feel bloated, constipated or blocked. Rehydrate with linseed tea. Practice going with the "flow" in life by using this releasing audio exercise on the website.

7am – 9am

Stomach related to: Mental anxiety, hypersensitivity and over empathy. Practice relaxation techniques before meals to calm digestion. Nourish the stomach at its peak time with a healthy and wholesome breakfast. Drink linseed tea to calm your adrenals and soothe anxiety.

9am – 11am

Spleen related to: Thoughts and intentions. Worry, anxiety and pensiveness will disturb the spleen.

Action: Use the relaxation exercise on the website to calm the mind and restore balance. Take a walk outside or do a meditation to calm your mental chatter.

11am – 1pm

Heart related to: Spirit and emotions. Ability to feel joy, love and peace.

Action: Practice deep breathing or the gratitude exercise on the resources page of the website at the high time of the heart. Breathe and be grateful for your life. Sit outside in the sun at between 11am – 1pm if you can, and allow yourself to accept the warmth and peace around you. Understand that you are part of something bigger.

1pm – 3pm

Small intestine related to: Judgement, discernment and decision making. The small intestine is the great separator. Also related to the heart.

Action: If you eat at this time ensure it is healthy and low in stress. Use the ADD and AVOID lists to release stress on the spleen. Practice taking decisions from a perspective of love and work on releasing judgements you hold around other people using the forgiveness exercise on the resources page of the website.

3pm – 5pm

Bladder related to: Fear, jealousy and suspicion. If you experience tiredness or depression during these hours your bladder could be out of balance.

Action: Drink warm water during these hours and write down or witness any negative emotions and hold the intention they will be eliminated with your urine.

5pm – 7pm

Kidneys related to: The energy inherited from your parents and your general constitution. In traditional Chinese medicine this is called your Jing J Also related to Courage, willpower and sexual potency.

Action: Remain hydrated with water and linseed tea to flush and soothe the kidneys. Use the relaxation exercise on the resources page of the website to combat stress.

7pm – 9pm

Pericardium related to: Physical and emotional protection of the heart. Connecting sex with physical love.

Action: Engage in loving sex. Love yourself and express who you are. Go to the resources page of the website and listen to the whole body exercise daily.

9pm – 11pm

Triple Burner Related to: Thorax (intake,) abdomen (transformation) and pelvis (elimination). The combination of these represents your ability to experience balance, joy and peace.

Action: Support the process of living and flourishing through good nourishment, exercise and relaxation. Choose techniques you feel drawn towards to manage cleansing and elimination.

In traditional Chinese medicine, energy travels through the body in two hourly windows. These two-hour windows are considered to be the high functioning time of the organs specified. If you experience a regular disturbance at a particular time for no apparent reason check the chart to find out which organ your energy is passing through at this time.

Where your body holds stagnation is likely to be a repeating pattern so it could be that a particular organ is struggling.

Check back through "The Story of You" and see if this resonates with your history or helps you understand your illness. Look for a technique that might support that area of your body. Send your healing intention to that area during your meditation or visualisation time.

If you have 8 hours sleep and still feel tired during the day or find yourself sneaking off for a nap, address your blood sugar. I was the queen of naps, but when I added linseed tea consistently to my diet, not only did my food cravings stop, but so did my need for a siesta!

Rule Number 3 – Remember...

Remember to Laugh

There might not appear to be much to laugh about right now. I know when I was ill, laughing was not top of my priority list! What I didn't know was how much I NEEDED to laugh and how laughter is a crucial part of any rebuild.

Laughter lightens our load in a way that nothing else does. It stops us taking ourselves, and our illness, so seriously, and even if just for a moment. In the middle of a real belly laugh, we feel our burden temporarily lifted. I'm not saying you should laugh off your symptoms. I'm saying laughter is an excellent distraction.

In the thirteenth century, surgeons started using laughter during operations for this very reason. Research shows that laughter reduces pain and stress-related hormones and boosts the immune system.

Whatever challenges you face, be they illness, redundancy, war, poverty, or divorce, they are all part of being human. We are here to have experiences and to grow from them. We are meant to be in a state of flux, constantly growing and developing. The easier we roll with the punches and focus on getting past them, the faster we tend to progress.

When a new challenge comes up for me, be it a symptom or some other signal from life, I try to get to the learning as soon as possible, knowing that once I get to the learning, the resolution will occur faster.

Take a minute to laugh at the ridiculousness of the situation you're in. Even if it's pain. Give in to it for a moment so you can ask what it's really about.

'It's not the challenge we face it's our response to it that counts.'

The pioneer of laughter therapy is widely regarded to be Norman Cousins, a respected American political journalist who believed that positive human emotions were the key to successfully fighting illness. Cousins battled heart disease and arthritis and was told his chances of survival were low. In response, he developed a recovery programme which used large doses of vitamin C combined with love, faith, hope and especially, laughter.

Here's what he learnt.

> 'I made the joyous discovery that ten minutes of genuine belly laughter had an anaesthetic effect and would give me at least two hours of pain-free sleep. When the pain-killing effect of the laughter wore off, we would switch on the motion picture projector again and not infrequently, it would lead to another pain-free interval.' – Norman Cousins.

Cousins' outlived all expectations and died in 1990, 10 years after his first heart attack and 36 years after his doctors first diagnosed his heart disease.

Laughter therapy or humour therapy as it is sometimes known, is now a recognised practice. It's also something you can easily incorporate into your rebuild. I make a point of watching or listening to something funny every day. Sometimes it's five minutes, sometimes it's fifty. What's important is that I get a loud belly laugh that instantly lifts my mood, and therefore my immune system. It also makes me randomly smile at any later point when I remember it.

Laughter makes you feel better about yourself and more at ease with the world around you and the effects of even a few minutes laughter can last for hours.

Try it. ☺

> 'Laughter makes the unbearable bearable, and a patient will a well-developed sense of humour has a better chance of recovery.' – **Bernie Siegel.**

The science behind laughter

According to the CTCA (Cancer Treatment Centers of America) laughter may help to:

- *Boost the immune system and circulatory system*

- *Enhance oxygen intake*

- *Stimulate the heart and lungs*

- *Relax muscles throughout the body*

- *Trigger the release of endorphins (the body's natural painkillers)*

- *Ease digestion/soothes stomach aches*

- *Relieve pain*

- *Balance blood pressure*

- *Improve mental functions (i.e., alertness, memory, creativity)*

- *Improve overall attitude*

- *Reduce stress/tension*

- *Promote relaxation*

- *Improve sleep*

- *Enhance quality of life*

- *Strengthen social bonds and relationships*

- *Produce a general sense of well-being*

(Source **http://www.cancercenter.com/treatments/laughter-therapy/**)

How to build laughter into your life?

Focus on happiness. Try watching, reading or listening to something funny every day. You can even recall funny events from your own life, jokes shared with friends, photos that make you smile or "You've been framed" moments you didn't capture on film.

Above all, decide to be happy. Make a conscious effort to find the positive in things. If you see someone who looks happy, emulate them. Try this for a day, a morning, an hour, or whatever you can manage. Notice if you experience resistance and write down why.

Remember to love

Love. It needs no introduction. It's why we're here and yet so many of us feel a lack of it somewhere in our lives.

You heard the expression "Love conquers all" and it does. Love can be healing and transformative. Being loved sends a "live" message to your cells. If you've ever fallen in love you remember how invincible you felt at this time.

I've never come across anyone madly in love with a chronic illness. So how about being in love with yourself and your life?

Here's what Dr Bernie Siegel says:

> 'I am convinced that unconditional love is the most powerful known stimulant of the immune system. If I told patients to raise their blood levels of immune globulins or killer T cells no one would know how. But if I can teach them to love themselves and others fully, the same changes happen automatically.'

Now I'm not saying go and have a wild love affair. I'm encouraging you to recognise, appreciate and return the love that is available in your life. The simple truth is that the more you focus on love, instead of a lack of love, the more love you create in your life. Notice it's as much about loving yourself as it is about loving others. When we deny ourselves the love and care we could give, we send a clear message that we deserve illness instead.

You can practise self-love through many of the exercises in this book. Listening and responding to your body is self-love. Understanding what this illness or condition is really about is self-love. Taking action is self-love. Nourishing and supporting yourself and devoting time to your health and wellbeing is self-love… you get the gist!

Self-love is devoting yourself to a patient you care deeply for, except this time the patient is you. Use this book and the practices within it to boost the love you feel, give to others and yourself and receive. No excuses. Section 6 has a powerful exercise to help you with this.

Enjoy ☺

Journal Space

SECTION 6

CREATING
THE NEW YOU

Now you'll work through an important step in moving towards wellness. This whole body experience is an exercise in becoming a better listener to your body. Be willing to see yourself in a whole new loving light and change your mindset around your health.

This section inspires you to remain alive to your potential. The simple message is this:

Change your thoughts change your results.

How many times have you looked at yourself and wished, even fleetingly, that you had the legs/ breasts/chest/arms/face of someone else? How often do you compare yourself to others with resignation and disappointment? You know this futile comparison to others makes you miserable, especially when you're feeling below par or have surgical scars to deal with. So, rather than indulging in your doubts about your physical worthiness, I'm going to take you through a powerful exercise to look at your own body in a whole new way.

If you feel resistance to this, note down which part of your body makes you feel uncomfortable, and why, and keep it to hand.

Find a full-length mirror (or as big a mirror as you have) in a warm, private room and take a few deep breaths. Close your eyes and centre yourself for a minute, breathing in through the nose and out through the mouth. If standing is uncomfortable, feel free to do this exercise sitting down. You can even sit in bed and do it.

Take your clothes off and without shame or blame cast your eyes over your body. Don't linger on any body part or dwell in any negativity, just note down which areas cause you discomfort to look at. It can be anything from stretch marks and scars to excess weight or weakness in an area.

Pay attention to the body part that bothers you and jot down what emotion comes up. Fear, anger, resentment, blame, shame – or something else? Whatever it is, write it down.

You're going to start over with your perception of your body, so it's important to witness everything that's currently blocking you from this. Without recognising it you can't release it, so be honest, this is just for you.

Close your eyes again and take a few more deep breaths. Remember back to the worksheets you have completed, to the story of you. Remember and honour what you've been through and understand that it has served a purpose in getting to this point.

Now imagine that you are changing the lenses of your eyes. Next time you open them you will see yourself only with love and acceptance. You will see your body as a vital part of you. Acknowledge that your body's only job is to keep you alive. That's all it knows how to do, and all it will try to do in any given moment regardless of the circumstances it finds itself in. That's why you're still here, reading this book.

So with your new loving lenses in, gently open your eyes and scan your body. Look at the areas of your body that make you uncomfortable. From a physical perspective acknowledge out loud the job that the particular body part is doing. Recognise how it is trying to serve you, to keep you alive. Turn the page to the list overleaf for inspiration.

Welcome the idea that you can choose to see your body in a whole new light. As you acknowledge each part that is connected to you, the greater whole, try to find some gratitude for how it tries to keep you alive and healthy, every day.

If you'd like to listen to an audio version of this process, go to the resources page of the website.

Seeing Yourself Differently: A Whole Body Exercise

As you read through this list focus on each area of your body. Really tune in, give it your attention and your gratitude for the service it provides to you.

Toes – They bend, straighten and balance me. When I want to reach up they support me. When I dance barefoot they grip and hold me. They wiggle in warm sand or a bubble bath, when I need to relax. They propel me when I am on the starting block. I dip my toes into the future every day, they represent the details of where I am going and who I am going to be.

Feet – They propel me forward and keep me balanced. They are my connection to the earth and to my understanding of myself and the life I am travelling through. By walking barefoot, I connect with nature and through them I jump for joy.

Ankles – They join my feet to my legs to allow me to move forward, both physically and in my life. They rotate to allow me to change direction when I need to. They represent flexibility and the grace with which I travel through life.

Legs – They carry me through life, whether running, dancing or at a slow amble. Strong and powerful they drive me forward into my future at the pace I choose. Swift, purposeful strides or slow and sensual, it's always my choice.

Knees – They represent my flexibility. They bend to allow me to sit and rest or walk and run. They creak and groan when I ask too much and kneel to surrender when I can no longer cope alone. Once "on my knees" I must ask for help and be willing to receive. They bend to pick up children and sit them on my knee. They relate to my ego, my sense of self and, if cared for wisely, they will climb any mountain that stands before me.

Bottom – The seat upon which I may rest, offering my legs relief when tired. The gentle curve of flesh that protects my pelvis from the rear and cushions me throughout life.

Genitals – The givers of life. The essence of masculinity and femininity. My self-worth or my self-destruction.

Hips – They are my balance. They carry a child within or balanced without as I sway to a gentle melody. They join my legs to my body, connecting my power to move with my inner core. They are creativity and the cradle through which life passes and energy is released.

Abdomen – This is my processing plant. It protects the organs that strengthen and detoxify me. It is bound by strong, deep muscles that wrap and protect my spine. It is my essential core, my mid-point and sense of power.

Stomach – My nourishment. My receptacle for new ideas and how I process and digest life. It feels strain where times are difficult. It feels satisfied and replete when times are good. It assimilates ideas and nutrients to strengthen me.

Breast/Chest – My nurturing centre. My heartbeat brings calm with its strong steady beat. My breast is a sanctuary for children and a resting pace for lovers. It is the balance of giving and receiving nourishment. My breast is both beauty and strength.

Lungs – The breath of my life, which I can choose to hold or release. I can make it easy or strained according to how I take life in and allow it to flow. My lungs take in the fullness of life if I let them.

Heart – The keeper of my soul. The centre of my love, my desires, my joy and bliss. It controls the flow of life through me according to my wishes. Free flowing and supple, or rigid and hardened, my heart is my connection to source and myself.

Back – My inbuilt support centre, without which everything crumbles. It holds me up every day and lays me down to rest at night. It bends, twists and turns for me and lets me know when I need to move and stretch. It is my safety. It is my past but it can only carry so much and care must be taken not to overburden it. My spine is my grace, my elegance, my stature. It always has my back.

Shoulders – They carry my experience of life. If I burden the weight of the world upon them they will ache. They are designed for lightness and agility. They are designed to roll to gently release what they can no longer carry.

Arms – They are how I embrace life. They are the wings I spread when I need to fly and the means to hold my experiences. They are the hug I give, the lover I hold, the warmth I wrap around myself.

Elbows – They are the joints that are always working. They give me flexibility and the opportunity to try new experiences. They represent change, curiosity and the flow with which I choose a new direction.

Wrists – They are the gracious, easy rotation that welcomes life as it enters through my palm. They are the support that balances me on my hands or pushes away from what I no longer need. They are my delicate strength or the flow of force.

Hands – They handle life for me and express my flow. They are my wave goodbye and my shake hello. They are the gentle touch that caresses my loved ones, soothes my child, and strokes my pet. They are the fists I bear in frustration and punch the sky with in celebration. They are a means of release, or the clutch and grasp that refuses to let go and keeps me stuck.

Fingers – They are my primary experience of touch and the delights of texture. They are the fingers I dip into the mixing bowl to test the cake batter. The digits I dip in the bath water to test the temperature and swirl the bubbles. They are the pinky that a baby's thumb curls around, the wearer of rings, the elegance of adornment, and the small details so easy to take for granted.

Neck – This represents my flexibility, my opportunity to turn and see things differently. My chance to change my perception. My neck gets stuck when I am locked in rigidity. It becomes stiff when a new perspective is needed. It holds my head proudly to the world and allows me to bow in gratitude, or it groans under the weight of my thoughts. My neck is graceful strength that requires ease to ensure I can consider my options and see what life has to offer.

Head/Brain – The programmer that creates a world to mirror my thoughts and beliefs. The base for my dreams, my hopes and ideas. It holds the thoughts that drive me towards action, or avoidance. It houses my reflexes and synapses, my powerhouse and control room. If I am brave enough to think differently, I can create a life I love and the health I desire.

Eyes – My vision. My ability to see clearly all that is past, present and yet to come. The mirror to my soul and the doorway to my hopes and the clarity that surrounds them. They see my potential long before I do.

Nose – My centre of smell and ability to breathe in all that life has to offer. The inhale of baking bread and freshly mown grass. The sneeze to expel something unwanted or threatening. The gentle whiff of my baby's scent, enticing fragrances, or the familiar smell of a lover. My recognition of life, myself, my loved ones and my worth.

Mouth – My smile. My kiss. My laughter and the lines to prove it. My opportunity to take in nourishment or refuse it. My willingness to speak or hold my silence. My gritted teeth or my relaxed jaw as I experience life.

Ears – My ability to receive sound. My music, internal or external. The crashing of waves or gentle morning birdsong. My still, small voice that whispers intuition to me if I am prepared to listen. They hear the love within life and seek to convey it to me. They are always open and listening for opportunities.

Voice – My expression of my self-worth, from a whisper to a shout. My generous laughter or my denial. My whoop of delight or my cry of pain. My whimper that remains when there is nothing left to say.

Face – The version of me that I show to the world. My mask or my truth, my joy and my pain. Always with me and only judgemental if I decide. It gifts me with lines to remember the laughter and seal the wisdom. It evolves as I change to reflect a life well lived and well loved. It is the means of recognition by which my loved ones know me. The face they look for in a crowd. The smile that means they are home.

What to remember?

As you work through the exercise, hold these intentions:

- *That you will see your body differently.*

- *That you will thank it for the service it provides.*

- *That you will nurture and care for it, in sickness and in health.*

– *That your relationship with it, and with yourself, from this point forward will be changed for the better.*

Understand that years of resentment or pain are hard to sweep away but not impossible. It's a question of choice, of shifting your perception until you feel a shift in your attitude.

If you get stuck on a particular body part, place your hand lightly upon it and make a connection with it. Acknowledge that it is part of you and, just as a branch cut off from the tree cannot grow, so a part cut off from the whole cannot heal.

Identify where the sticking point is in your perception. What are you not bringing to this situation to change the way you feel? What are you not releasing?

Be mindful of your reaction to this exercise. What emotion does it bring up? Sadness? A need to re-connect? Grief? A need to forgive yourself?

Understand that you cannot get to health from your current perception of illness, you must come FROM a perception of yourself as healthy, or in the process of becoming healthy.

Releasing Trapped Emotions

To allow the emotion to move through and out of you, you first need to recognise and accept it. Allow yourself to look it square in the eye and acknowledge it exists, then make a conscious decision to release it, in the name of your rebuild.

You are not denying the emotion of the pain it's caused you, you are simply choosing not to let it affect you in the same way, from this point forward. This is a practice to repeat over and over. By choosing release you are moving towards health. By choosing to hold onto the emotion you will remain stuck.

Re-affirm your release of this emotion out loud by saying:

I accept that I feel… about… and while I may not know why this has happened, I know it is part of something much bigger, better and healthier for me and for this reason I am willing to accept it in this moment and release it entirely to make room for something AMAZING.

Repeat as often as required.

A big part of rebuilding is removing toxicity in all forms and creating the space for healing to occur. Nature abhors a vacuum and by choosing to fill the void with love and healing you are supporting yourself on the path to wellness.

Look at your body once more, scan from toe to head, as you read this message from your body to you. Scan again with loving and grateful eyes.

A Message to You from Your Body

I have been entrusted to you for this lifetime. I will always do my best to keep you safe and protect you. When you are cut, I will heal you. When you are cold, I will send blood to your core to keep your vital organs warm. When you are in pain I will produce endorphins to ease your suffering. I will only create disease as a last resort. I wholeheartedly support your recovery. If you support me I will always repair you. I want you to live. I want you to flourish. I respond to your joy, your love, your every thought.

Close your eyes and open your heart as you breathe deeply and fully for a whole minute. Let this message in. Let your cells feel your intention to heal, to be well. Let the feeling of love spread to every cell in your body and especially to those areas where your perception needed to shift.

Why should I do this?

Use this powerful opportunity to change the way you view yourself and motivate you to take good care of yourself. This is the beginning of self-love, the most powerful healing tool of all.

Well done for making it this far. Up to now, you've covered a lot of ground on your nutritional and physical rebuild. This is what I like to call "The Outer Work". Now it's time for the "Inner work" and this, as I learnt through my own rebuild, is just as important. Prepare to blow your mind as you move onto the mental game of rebuilding in section 7.

Journal Space

SECTION 7

MINDING YOUR HEALTH

'The word incurable, which is so frightening to so many people, really only means that the particular condition cannot be cured by "outer" methods and that we must GO WITHIN to effect the healing.' – Louise Hay

How you use your mind to rebuild your health is as important as how you nourish and cleanse your body. The thoughts and beliefs you hold affect your body at a cellular level and determine your ability to achieve true and lasting health. In this section, I'll give you exercises to train your mind and tools that are life skills for longevity. In this section, you will learn to see things differently and visualise the health you really desire and deserve.

If it's new to you, the world of illness can feel like an ongoing assault. You just want to get your head above the parapet but then something else sets you back. I got to a point where I thought I'd lost health altogether. I began to believe I'd never be well again.

If you're holding a similar belief, it can easily turn into a thought pattern and ultimately into a reality. It took me years to learn how to change my perception and use the most powerful tool in my rebuild arsenal (my mind,) to my advantage.

Your most powerful tool

If you think you got to this point through physical symptoms alone, think again. Your mental and emotional thoughts and beliefs manifest in physical symptoms over a period of time. This is how your body communicates with you.

Many people are actually creating the blocks to their own good health without even realising it. To try and treat the physical without shifting the mental is a losing game. Now it's time to get out of your own way and stop being the obstacle to your own healing.

If this sounds a little mad then, like me, you're probably the kind of person who needs to see some tangible proof before you can buy into a concept. So here's a quick exercise to demonstrate the effects of your mental process upon your health:

    – *Get a physical or mental picture of someone you love deeply and unconditionally and who loves you back. It can be a friend, a lover, a child, a parent or even a pet. The key is that this person (or animal) brings you joy and you look forward to seeing and spending time with them. Look at their picture or hold their image in your mind's eye and let the feeling of love and happiness wash over you. Feel yourself respond. Perhaps you're even smiling now?*

Congratulations you've just boosted your immunity. Feels good doesn't it?

    – *Now do the opposite. Picture someone who annoys you. Perhaps you disagree with them over something, or whenever they walk in the room it's like chalk scraping down a blackboard. Hold them in your mind's eye and notice that when you think of them your energy drops. You feel this subtle shift in even at a cellular level.*

Now imagine feeling frustrated or angry with someone or something for days, weeks, months, years. Some people project anger, blame and even hate towards other people, organisations, historical events and even objects, for decades. This energy or input has to have a physical output and guess what, it rarely affects the person being hated but it ALWAYS affects the one doing the hating. This build-up of toxic emotion must have a physical effect and this manifests as ill health.

Don't believe me?

Science has proved that our thoughts really do affect every cell in our body. We live under the common misconception that the mind is in the brain, or at least in the head. Which is why when someone is labelled mentally unstable, or "out of their mind", we take a finger and roll it around close to our temple to signify their craziness.

In actual fact, the mind is in EVERY cell in our body and every cell responds to the stimulus we give it. When you feel something, your cells feel it and react. Even your genes respond to your conscious and unconscious thoughts, emotions and beliefs, as the study of epigenetics has proved.

But there are people and things in my life that piss me off!

Isn't that a great part of the human experience.

You know, while it's nice to think we could all interact only with the people, places and things that make us happy, the truth is that life is a journey and like any road trip, there will be bumps along the way. Irritations, traumas, bereavements, betrayal, these are all part and parcel of life.

So how can you deal with this when you are re-building yourself? You use your perception.

The circumstances don't change. Your thinking about the circumstances changes.

Whether it's a person, an event or trauma that's affecting your thoughts, the shift has to come from within. It's always an inside job. Don't waste time expecting an external shift to make you well. Only an internal shift can do that.

Currently, you perceive something according to your beliefs. If you believe all dogs are dangerous, when you see a dog you will think it's dangerous and act accordingly by freezing, panicking or running away.

The trick is to change what you believe, then your thoughts and behaviour also change. The hard part is that many of your beliefs will have been formed in childhood or earlier so you may not have consciously made a choice to hold a particular belief, but you feel the effects of it all the time.

Here's an example

When I was at my most ill, I could barely walk more than 100m without needing to lie down. I had been an active sportswoman prior to being ill and I loved nothing more than a vigorous bike ride, a high impact dance class or a week of full throttle skiing.

While I was ill, I got to a point where I truly believed I would never be able to do any of those things again. I grieved for this part of myself on a daily basis. It made me feel terrible. I struggled to accept I would never be well again, but that's what the evidence, or my circumstances, seemed to be telling me.

As my exhaustion and symptoms persisted over the months and years, I began to lose the memory of what it felt like to be well. I could no longer imagine how it felt to be energised and for me this was the danger zone.

As the famous saying goes:

> 'If the mind can conceive it, the mind can achieve it.'

I knew that if I couldn't even conceive it, or the hold the image of health and vitality in my mind, then there was sure as hell no way I'd ever fully recover.

At the time, I didn't know how to get out of this vicious cycle but I was aware that my thoughts turned from healing to simple self-preservation. I just wanted to stay alive.

I settled into a coping strategy of survival while secretly wondering if I was slowly dying. When I had the chance to go and do something even vaguely active, I declined. I no longer believed it was possible for me. My beliefs were that I shouldn't push myself as I couldn't risk feeling worse. So my beliefs changed my behaviour.

The result?

A lot of time not doing things I would have enjoyed, that probably would have helped me feel better.

How can I change my beliefs?

Simple – accept the diagnosis not the prognosis.

> Only you can decide what the diagnosis means to you. Only you can create a belief around what's possible for you.

When people are told they only have 6 weeks left to live, typically they die sooner. Why? They place all their belief in the prognosis. I'm not saying deny the diagnosis – that just tells you what's going on in your body – but the prognosis is what you will make of it and that's totally up to you.

Follow the example of Morty Lefkoe* who was told he had cancer, but decided not to give his diagnosis or prognosis any meaning. With no meaning attached to the cancer, he could create no fear around it. In the absence of fear, all he had to do was set about healing it. Within 99 days Morty moved from a cancer diagnosis to tests indicating he was cancer free.

He treated cancer like a broken leg. Yes, it needed to be treated but he was not overwhelmed and he did not treat the diagnosis as serious. These days he maintains the diet and lifestyle changes he adopted as part of his healing regime and he's still certain he's going to be absolutely fine.

*http://www.mortylefkoe.com/

What you need to know

- *Your beliefs control your thoughts*

- *Your thoughts control your actions*

- *Your actions control your behaviour*

- *Your behaviour controls your results*

To rebuild and maintain good health you have to wholeheartedly believe it's possible in the first place. Otherwise, all your best efforts will be sabotaged.

A Few Words on Cancer

It's. Not. A. War.

Have you noticed how the advertising around cancer has changed? These days it's all about waging war on cancer. As though cancer is some alien force that has invaded us and must be blasted out. As though aggressive approaches like chemotherapy are the best option, or even the only, option.

> *When you picture your body as the enemy the only person you're only doing battle against is yourself.*

Don't hate the cancer or yourself. Instead, see the part of you that is toxic, in pain or suffering, as a fragmented part of your greater whole. It needs to be reconnected to you and loved. You do not need to attack yourself to heal. Shift into this mindset and your recovery has already begun.

But my doctor says...

If you are being treated by someone who sees you as a symptom, or a prognosis that cannot be changed rather than a person, then it's time to help them change their perception, or change your caregiver.

I'm scared of my treatment plan.

If you are in a situation where you are facing your own mortality and the fear is all consuming then above all else, read *Love, Medicine and Miracles* by Bernie Siegel and consider that the drugs and chemotherapy you might be opposed to might buy you some extra rebuild time.

See standard medical treatments like radiotherapy, chemotherapy and surgery as tools you are using to support yourself, while you figure out how to change, rebuild, heal and live. If you are terrified of chemotherapy and think of it as poison, you may well prove yourself right.

Negative programming around chemotherapy is enough to convince anyone it will be a terrible experience but many patients who have the right outlook, information and support, don't always experience side effects. A positive attitude to whichever therapy you choose is key, so manage your perceptions carefully and embrace whichever therapies you choose.

Changing Your Perception About What's Possible

A physical shift creates a mental shift.

If you do the practices in the book your physicality will strengthen and boost your resilience. Use even a small amount of physical improvement as a demonstration that your health is improving.

Just as when you plant an acorn it takes time to become an oak tree, now you are planting the seeds of good health, but you need to be patient, to allow them to germinate.

Remind yourself daily that you are in the process of rebuilding. You are creating an alternative to illness and this is what it looks like while along the way. It is not perfect, it is a process. Good health is a journey. Thinking this way takes the pressure off you and quietens your ego, which wants to keep you stuck in fear and ill health.

A mental shift creates a physical shift.

Read about people who've recovered from, overcome or survived the symptoms, disease or condition you have.

Read the book or watch the movie *The Secret*. Find more info on the resources page of my website.

Astound yourself with people who've achieved miraculous recoveries. Get into the vibration of health and understand that we are all given the same essential piece of kit – the human body – and what's possible for one is possible for all.

In every moment, we can choose to create health. On the following page, you'll find some exercises to help you.

Exercises to Create Health

1. Positive action changes perception

    If you can't THINK positive, DO something positive. Exercise, call a friend or your support buddy, put on a happy song (have a CD or playlist on hand) reach for something inspirational – the vision statement you'll create later in this section is ideal. Make an impromptu list of everything you're grateful for. Send a text, email or letter of appreciation to a friend telling them how great they are.

2. Teach yourself a new truth

    Work through this as often as you need to.

    –   *What am I thinking right now about a particular person, event or circumstance?*

    –   *What does this mean I believe?*

    –   *Is this belief I'm holding actually true? Look at all the evidence in the world that disproves your belief. For example: are there people who've rebuilt themselves from hideous and horrible circumstances and changed their lives and their health for the better? (The answer is yes).*

    –   *Are there people who've experienced miraculous recoveries simply by the power of changing their thinking? (Again, yes).*

    –   *So does this prove it's possible to change my beliefs? (Yes, yes yes!).*

    –   *What will I choose to think instead?*

    –   *What new belief will I have to create to make this happen?*

3. Be willing to see things differently

    When I was struggling with beliefs that had a real hold on my life, I turned to my mentor, Mary Morrissey and in her work I would always find these words:

    'How can you see this differently?'

    This question alone proved transformative for me and it allowed me to bring truth into the areas where I needed to change.

    Make a commitment to bring more truth into the areas in your life where you feel you are struggling. Once you get to the truth you're currently holding behind the belief then consciously choose again. It's as simple as saying "I am willing to see this differently".

    Allow a new truth to present itself then write out the new belief and settle into it. Revisit it three times today and pin it up or put it somewhere where you will see it frequently over the next 21 days.

    When you deal with other people involved in this issue be sure to act from your new truth. If the people involved used to drive you crazy, you will find, in the presence of your new truth, their lack of truth eventually ceases to exist. All you have to do is hold your course and stay true to your truth.

Losing Your Labels

How many people do you know with a health label? I'm allergic, I'm intolerant of X, I'm diabetic, I've got X.

Labels are what doctors assign to patients in order to treat them. They match the symptoms the person presents to the title of a condition in order to partner them with a medication they've been trained to administer.

For example, an inhaler is usually the treatment for asthma. Anti-histamines are the treatment for allergies. Chemotherapy is one of the treatments for cancer. You get the picture.

I understand that this approach is helpful, perhaps even necessary, for the medical profession, but it also validates the patient's symptoms and complaints. It creates a belief in them and they go home and say, 'I've got…' or, 'I'm allergic to…' The trouble is twofold. First, it removes choice. People assume they'll ALWAYS be diabetic, allergic or whatever it is they're carrying around, from that point forward. Second, people get lost in their labels. They live with them. They allow the label to become a part of their life rather than a temporary state they're passing through on their way to health. They make it welcome so to speak and eventually, they begin to define themselves and what's possible for them, according to their label. And many of them have more than one.

I believe accepting a label and shutting off from your own potential is a definite contributor to disease. If you let yourself become the illness, symptom or condition, you cannot become truly healthy.

As it says in *A Course in Miracles*,

> *'The vision of one world costs you the vision of the other.'*

If you truly believed, you could be healthy, your choices would drive you to attain that state.

Give me an example.

I was diagnosed with asthma at 24 years old. I was hospitalised and put on a nebulising machine so that I could breathe and sometime later, I was sent home, with an inhaler and told that I was asthmatic. If you've ever experienced an asthma attack, or any situation where you can't breathe for that matter, you will understand how terrifying it can be. I did not want to experience that ever again so I took on that label "asthmatic" and I acted in a way that felt responsible, but was totally based in fear.

For years afterwards, I didn't dare leave the house without my inhaler. And if I did, I would turn right around to go home and get it. Asthma felt like a threat to my survival. Asthma had all the power and I was paralysed with fear.

It took me years of learning, but as I re-built myself I began to notice that I used my inhaler less and less. I would forget to take it with me and I wouldn't panic. In rebalancing my body I didn't experience the symptoms that caused me to need an inhaler and eventually I forgot I owned them.

Several years ago, I found a couple of inhalers at the back of a cupboard I was clearing out. They were both seriously out of date as I hadn't used or needed an inhaler in ten years. I took stock of how grateful I was to be healthy and then, with a huge smile, I threw those inhalers away. I'm not asthmatic.

Consider what labels you have been given, or given yourself. Here's an exercise to help you see them differently:

Exercise: Losing your labels

- *Write out the labels you've been given or you've given yourself. Note down anything emotional that relates to them e.g. "I'm a terrible mother" or "she's a lazy good-for-nothing" are just as relevant as "I'm allergic to nuts" or "I'm always tired".*

- *Write down how your labels have or are reducing your potential. Remember it's not about denying the facts (you might genuinely explode if you eat shellfish right now,) it's about denying the power of the facts to control your life.*

Think of it this way. Labels disconnect you from your body. You assign the label to part of your body and then perceive that body part as diseased, bad, infected, or something equally negative. Most fundamentally, you begin to see that part of your body as separate from the rest of you. You stop trusting it.

Think about, and notice, how you describe your labels to others.

Here's just some of the things I used to hear myself say:

- *'My lungs really let me down.'*

- *'My liver can't cope.'*

- *'I can't think straight. My brain is screwed.'*

- *'My Adrenals are shot to pieces.'*

- *'My blood sugar is a disaster.'*

- *'The dark circles under my eyes are so ugly.'*

- *'I can't exercise right now.'*

- *'My thyroid doesn't work properly.'*

Each statement, each belief I held about my body and my health, came directly from a place of negativity and judgement. There is nothing in any of the sentences above that supported me into health. In every instance, I was the victim. That's why I had to learn to lose my labels. That's why you have to learn to lose your labels.

Labels are a reflection of your belief system. If you ultimately think you'll never recover, then you'll adopt, create and use labels that ensure your body gets the message that it should remain ill. You are a co-creator of your own experience. You get to decide how long you're going to define your life with labels.

If you don't think your labels are weighing you down, do the following exercise.

Exercise: How your labels affect you

- *Get a selection of tin cans (about 10–15 should do it) and a couple of carrier bags.*

- *Look back over your list labels. Add new ones as they occur to you.*

- *For every label, pick up a tin can, put it into a carrier bag and hold the bag. Say each label out loud as you pick up the can and place it in the bag. Witness the belief system you're subjecting yourself to.*

- *When you have gone through all your labels and you have a selection of cans in your bags, notice the extra weight you feel. It might feel heavy or light depending on how honest you've been with yourself. If you've only got two cans in a bag, you're kidding yourself. We've ALL got labels and we create new ones on a regular basis.*

- *Feel the weight of the cans. They represent the burden you are metaphysically lugging around with you all day. If you don't believe me, try carrying the bags around for the rest of the day. It would be inconvenient, to say the least.*

- *As you put the bags down repeat out loud:*

I'm willing to lose my labels. I'm ready to let go of my old beliefs about what's possible for me and create a healthy future.

But I don't know who I am without my labels?

When you're dependent on a label it can be hard to let go. For you it may mean there's no excuse not to get better. Losing your labels means really facing what's causing your illness and actually dealing with it.

Sounds hard, but trust me, it is the only way to get the health and the life you want.

Go back and look at your list of labels. Next to each label, write down the body part that you have stopped trusting. Ask yourself this key question: How can I see this differently? Yes, you may have symptoms, pain and a scary diagnosis, but in the midst of that you still have a choice, and you always will. As you look at your labels, think how you could reframe them.

Could you go from 'I'm exhausted' to 'I'm gradually getting stronger'?

How about changing 'I've got cancer' to 'I'm listening to my body and I'm in the process of rebuilding myself'?

Here are some examples of how I re-framed my labels:

'My lungs really let me down – My lungs are telling me to relax and breathe life in while I alkalise so they can heal.'

'My liver can't cope – I'm taking the stress off my liver so it can clear out toxins and make me stronger.'

'My blood sugar is a disaster – I am stabilising my blood sugar a little more each day.'

'The dark circles under my eyes make me look so bad – This is what it looks like while I'm getting better, so I forgive myself.'

'My thyroid doesn't work properly – My thyroid's doing its best so I'll do my best to support it.'

A key phrase to use is 'This is what it looks like while…' Use this for each statement if it helps you see your condition or symptom differently even if it's as simple as 'This is what it looks like while I'm rebuilding myself'.

Try this out and notice the shift you experience as a result.

Take a tip from cancer survivors

In Bernie Siegel's book *Love, Medicine and Miracles*, he found that people who survived cancer approached it from a different mindset. Right from the outset, they focussed on what they would be doing once they recovered and set about doing those things before they recovered. A sort of "why wait" approach. They acted as though they were going to live and they didn't get stuck in the mindset of disease.

Similar to Morty Lefkoe, they accepted the diagnosis but denied the prognosis and set about reframing it as the road to recovery.

Slip into the survivor's mindset and ask yourself – How can I see this differently?

If you knew you were going to survive and be well, what would you start doing today?

Exercise: Choosing LOVE instead of your labels

This is a little yogi trick recommended by author Gabby Bernstein. If you need a physical reminder every time you use your labels, you'll love this!

- *Place an elastic band around your wrist. Every time you think about, or talk about your labels, pull the elastic gently back and let it snap back against your skin. It will sting! Not quite a slap in the face but definitely something to stop you and make you re-think*

- *Once you've stopped yourself mid-thought you need to choose a different thought instead. ALWAYS choose something loving.*

- *Think a kind, loving thought about the part of your body that's communicating with you, that's trying to heal, that's asking for care. Don't debate about it, don't deny it or dwell on it, just do it.*

- *Even if you can't think of anything positive, simply say 'I choose love instead'.*

I'd feel stupid doing that

Great! Lighten up! If you haven't truly felt loving towards yourself in a while this will take you out of your comfort zone and that's where the magic happens!

Laugh at yourself a bit more. You remember how important it is to laugh? Love yourself more. Love's crazy and silly and all those fun things but one thing I know for sure is, love never lowers your IQ or your immunity. ☺

Vision Your Health

What the mind can conceive the body can achieve.

Can you create a picture in your mind of the health you want?

Can you get a sense of how great health would feel in your body? Can you create that sensation in your mind and hold a mental picture you can refer back to?

If you have always been unwell or had a particular symptom or condition, can you find someone who's recovered and read about their journey and success?

Visualising what you want and involving all of your senses is one of the fastest ways to make it happen. Your mind is the most powerful tool you have and this is a fantastic way to use it.

Here's a visualisation exercise for you to use. To listen to a recorded version of this exercise, please go to the resources page of the website.

Visualisation Exercise:

Close your eyes for a moment and give yourself permission to indulge in a sensory experience of your own creation.

Take a couple of deep breaths, relax and let the day around you slip away for a few moments.

Inhale deeply and test your senses. Conjure up images in your mind to help you. Can you smell a pine forest? How about freshly cut grass?

Listen closely. Can you hear rain on a tin roof? The roll of waves onto the shore? The cheer of a crowd?

Now imagine plunging your hands into warm sand, can you feel that sensation in your mind? Imagine running your fingers across the softness of a sheepskin rug or sinking into a warm bath.

Can you taste a mint humbug? Vanilla ice cream? The crack of popcorn in your mouth?

Imagine a mountain in front of you, covered in glistening white snow.

Be aware that your senses are creating this experience for you. Make the images clearer and more colourful. Use all five senses.

Imagine you're on a beach watching a beautiful sunset. Feel the warmth of the sun's last rays on your face. Wiggle your toes in the sand. Hear the waves lapping gently. Smell sunscreen on your skin. Immerse yourself into this moment.

Now turn your awareness to your health and keep breathing deeply. Allow yourself to imagine what it would feel like to be symptom-free?

Don't listen to any thoughts or judgements that pop up and tell you it's not possible. Just imagine how your body would feel if you were fit and healthy.

What would your day be like?

How would your body look?

How would your body feel?

What would your new healthy life be like?

Where would you go?

What would you do?

Who would you speak to?

How much joy can you let yourself experience as you mentally go through this scenario?

Now transfer that imagery to the page and create a tool you can use every day to bring health within your reach. It's time to use your pen to change your perception!

Exercise: Creating your health vision

You're going to create a blueprint of the health you would love, and as you do so, remember three things:

1. Date it three years from now. (See explanation below)

2. Keep it present tense. Write it as though it's happening now.

3. Keep it positive. State what you do want rather than what you don't i.e. I feel strong enough to go to the gym, rather than, I don't want to feel exhausted all the time.

Vision the quality of health so much that it begins to live in you on a permanent basis. Notice health all around you in nature. Look for healthy people and animals. Focus on their energy and wellness and you create a subtle shift that tells your unconscious to produce the same. Vibrate at the frequency of health that can be found in the simplest forms, everywhere you look.

Use this worksheet to create the health vision you desire. Feel into it, use all your senses, make it as real as possible as you write it.

It's …………………………………….. (Date three years from now)

I wake up feeling…

I jump out of bed and…

I am so grateful for…

When I see myself in the mirror I feel…

I love my body because…

My body feels…

I love being able to exercise. Every day, I enjoy…

I nourish my body with…

As I prepare my breakfast, I smell…

As I prepare lunch, I touch…

As I enjoy my evening meal, I taste…

I love my life because…

I am so grateful for my family and friends who support my health choices. Always finish with – This or something better, thank you.

I feel stupid

Approach it another way.

Ask yourself, who would I be without this illness? Write it down.

Ask yourself how would I hold myself?

How would I speak?

How would I move?

How would I nourish myself and love myself?

Become visionary is an asset you can use over and over again. Get creative.

Writing it down doesn't work for me.

If images rather than words work better for you then create pictures in your mind of the health you want and find images that represent it. Use them to create a mood board that you look at every day. Translate the feeling in all of your senses to your body so rather than saying I want to look like "that person", imagine how it would feel in YOUR body to look that healthy.

As you immerse yourself in the images, use all your senses to feel, smell, touch, taste and hear what your life would be like if the things on your mood board were actually happening right now in your body and in your life. Study that mood board as if you are living that healthy, successful life and allow yourself to switch fully into that frequency.

How often should I use this?

At least once a day for 5–10 minutes, but the more you can engage your senses in this exercise the faster you can bring it into reality. The key is to really feel it in every cell of your being.

I'm not sure I believe this.

'Everything is created twice.' Mary Morrissey.

Look around you. Everything you can see or touch was once a thought in someone's mind before it was created as a thing. Everything starts as an idea in someone's mind before it's brought into being. Every chair, table, car, laptop, iPad, story in a book, programme on TV and anything else you can think of, started as an idea.

Ideas are the currency of the universe.

In other words, you cannot create great health unless you can imagine it and hold a picture in your mind of what great health would look and feel like for you.

Why do I have to date it in the future?

It's a trick you can play on your mind. One year is not long enough and your reasoning mind will throw up too much objection about what's possible for you. Whereas in three years, even your reasoning mind knows it cannot limit what might be possible for you and so it doesn't bother trying.

Always remember to start with your date as three years from now.

Can I add in bits that aren't about my health?

Of course. Go for it! Focus on your health first and then expand it to the rest of your life when you feel comfortable. Imagine doing meaningful, rewarding work you love. Imagine helping other people. Imagine using your skills and talents to be of service to others, or the world in general.

Use this exercise to get clear on what you would love in every area of your life, and why.

I'm struggling to imagine myself healthy and strong.

I understand that when you've been ill for a length of time, it's easy to forget you've ever been well. It may feel as though you've never truly been strong and healthy. The good news is you don't need to remember from experience here. You can create from your desire for health.

Find an image that represents the health you want and use that. Find words to describe what you see, or what's appealing about the kind of healthy body you want and incorporate them into your worksheet.

You can also use a trick I learnt from Dr Jean Houston, best-selling author and luminary in the field of personal development. Jean claims that while she isn't a writer, she is a great cook. Cooking is a passion of hers. It's an area she feels strong in. So when she wants to communicate with millions of people and knows a book is the best way, she puts on her chef's hat and approaches the writing as a recipe. She knows the ingredients she has to put in and how it has to be mixed together to create a compelling read that will help millions of people. She writes as a chef, rather than as a writer.

I used this in my own rebuild. I wasn't a born healer, miracle worker or physician, so in my mind I lacked the power to make myself better. What I was really good at though, was studying. I love learning and so I engaged this "keen student" aspect of my personality and took on my health as my project.

I read avidly, studied many different theories and techniques and applied them. There was no Eureka moment where I leapt up and said 'That's it, I'm cured', but there were many mini-miracle moments where I realised what was happening, and finally had the information do something about it.

To this day, I still love to learn and I actually enjoy sitting exams. The student is an element of my personality I feel strong and confident in. By applying it to my illness, I could generate enough critical mass to make a change.

To try this in your life, find an area that you feel strong in, or have historically felt successful in. It might be that you're a great negotiator and can use this part of your personality to manage the Add and Avoid sections of nutrition. It might be that you're a great cook and coming up with new and exciting healthy recipes can be a real source of pleasure and health for you and your family.

It might be that you're an engineer and you can use your technical brain to understand what's happening in your body and how you can support it as a system. Think about how the qualities and skills you possess in this area can be applied to creating health instead of illness. Write down how to transfer these skills to achieve your aim.

Now you are well on the way to health and in section 8 it's time to address the seven biggest blocks likely to sabotage your efforts and keep you from health.

Journal Space

SECTION 8

THE 7 BIGGEST BLOCKS TO GREAT HEALTH

So what's really stopping you from experiencing vibrant health? If you want to know the truth, this is the section where you'll find out.

From dealing with fears, whether real or subconscious to overcoming the ego, by the end of this section you'll understand that everything is a choice. More importantly, you'll have the tools to support you in health, instead of keeping you locked in illness.

This section helps you to remove the final barriers to your wellness and vitality and includes what I consider to be one of the most important parts of this book – getting to the "Gift" in your illness.

Getting to the Gift allows you to see why you needed this experience in the first place and what message it has for your life. I believe there is a purpose and value in every experience, good or bad, and the sooner we understand this, the sooner we can move through the experience of illness and choose health instead.

> *Don't seek for health, seek for your barriers to health. It's not about finding great health it's about releasing the blocks to allowing it in your life.*

Following the process in this book, you can change the way you nourish yourself, you can support your body in its detox role and facilitate a cleansing process. You can work with your thoughts and beliefs around what's possible for your health and still there might be something holding you back from health.

It's you.

The truth is, great health isn't something you have to go out and find. It already exists. Your body is programmed to heal and be healthy. Your task is to release the blocks to allowing health into your life. Let's get started…

Block No 1 – Fear

I believe fear is our second strongest emotion, right behind love. It lives deep within our mind, so that's where we have to go to clear it out. Just as the techniques we discussed earlier in the book support you through a physical detox, this section is to support you through a mental and emotional detox.

The problem is never what you think, it's your belief in what you think and the power you give to that belief.

What's your greatest fear?

If you're spending most of your time focussing on it, the chances are you're creating it.

My greatest fear was death. I got to a point where that seemed inevitable and it was pretty preoccupying. I felt so unwell and had all the tests, scans, X-rays and MRIs that doctors could throw at me, without any real conclusion. I decided I had something deep and insidious that was slowly killing me and after I had died they would perform an autopsy and declare they found a rare condition that was to blame.

Finally, my doctor told me she could see how ill I was, but she didn't know what else to do. When she handed me a prescription for Prozac, as though I could numb myself through my illness until my inevitable end, something in me clicked. I handed her back the prescription and thanked her for all she'd tried to do. She seemed to have confirmed my greatest fear. There was nothing anyone could do. It was at this point that I wrote the letter to my children that I shared with you earlier in the book.

It was the hardest thing I've ever done but something HUGE happened for me the day I wrote that letter. I surrendered. I gave up trying to control my illness. I gave up what felt like a battle I couldn't win. I'm a spiritual, not a religious person and at that point, I handed it over to something higher than myself and said, I can't do this anymore, you take over.

The Power of Surrender

To completely surrender is a powerful exercise because you agree to whatever comes next. You relinquish all control. You become teachable.

The beauty of surrender, as I learnt, is that it creates a sense of freedom. After the trauma of writing the letter, I was lighter. I had done what I felt I needed to do. I had made provision for my children and now I would wait and see what life had in store, whether that would be death or something else.

The interesting thing was that whereas before I had focussed so much energy on being ill, now that I had handed it over, I no longer felt the need to do that. The sense of space this created allowed me to consider alternatives. By not focussing constantly on illness, I had time to focus on something else. Ideas dropped in and when after one week, then two, then three, I was still alive, I thought, *Well, okay, if I'm going to be here for a bit longer, maybe I should try out something else…*

A friend mentioned a Chinese herbalist and I paid attention. I went along and started to learn and apply what she taught me. I met another alternative practitioner and started to learn and apply. I experienced small improvements each time and because I had shifted my focus, I started to hope.

Slowly but surely, I spent the next ten years experiencing, studying and learning first hand from a series of amazing holistic practitioners and teachers around the world. By putting down the burden of ill health, I had been able to pick up something else – the possibility of my own potential to rebuild myself. I had arrived at my fork in the road and made a choice to stop being afraid of death.

Exercise: Finding your fear and dealing with it

If you prefer to listen to this exercise, go to the resources page of the rebuild website.

Get comfy and take a few deep breaths. What's your biggest fear?

Look for one that creates an immediate reaction. A physical reaction in your body. It could be anything from anguish, anxiety or panic to grief or loss.

Sit with it for anything up to two minutes. If it gets too strong, rather than seeing yourself in it, imagine it playing on an iPad in your hands. If it's still too disturbing, turn the volume down on the iPad, so you see the images but there's no sound. You can even make the picture smaller if you want to.

Once you've sat with the fear for two minutes, try and identify the feeling behind this fear.

For example, if your biggest fear is death, then is it really about you dying or is it about leaving your kids without a mother/father?

If your biggest fear is your lover leaving you, is it really about losing him/her, or is it about being alone?

Fear is emotion heading in the wrong direction. If you can get to the hidden message in your feelings, you have a good shot at turning fear around.

Try to identify the real feeling that your fear is masking.

Is your fear about something happening to you or someone else?

If it's about you:

Are you afraid of dying, someone leaving you, or losing something because of your illness? (Fear is usually based around separation of some sort).

If it's about someone else:

Are you afraid of losing them or being separated somehow? Are you afraid of being left or abandoned?

Close your eyes and step into this fear for a second. Where do you feel it in your body?

Imagine you have a magnifying glass that can see through flesh and bone. Zoom into the part of your body where the fear is being held. What does it look like?

If you could have a tool, device or even a superpower which you could use to heal the area and return it to normal functioning, what would you choose?

Imagine this is given to you. Whether it's a tool you use all the time, something you've just invented or a blast of super healing white light, see the area of your body receiving it now.

Is there anything else the area needs? If yes, see it being received. If no, say aloud:

> *I release this fear and everything connected with it, from my body. I thank it for the learning it has provided. I give it permission to leave and I ask that it be replaced with love.*

Remember fear is just emotion heading in the wrong direction.

This is not a miracle cure but a process. Use it each time the fear comes up. If you practice this exercise often enough, you will begin to notice that even when something small flares up for you, you can quickly assess the feeling beneath the fear and ask, 'What's this really about?'

You will start to see patterns emerge and as you realise this is all part of the same message formed by an untrue belief, you will be able to take the sting out of the fear and watch it fade from your life.

My experience with fear

As a result of being abused as a child, I grew up with a very strong belief that the world wasn't a safe place and adults couldn't be trusted. This played out as fearful behaviour that was rash, illogical and, at times, rude. My fear was telling me I needed to go back and release some childhood trauma. Once I'd done this (and believe me, it was a practice I engaged in, over a period of time), I noticed the peace I felt in the place of fear. I just felt happier to be in the world.

If you've never considered communicating with your body or aspects of your subconscious that can help you with information, this may all sound a little wacky. So let me ask you this:

What have you got to lose?

At worst you'll feel silly and laugh at yourself. At best, you'll get some answers that allow you to shift the fear that's holding you back.

If we don't work on our fears we stay stuck in them, and guess what? They grow. A small fear left unchecked can quickly spiral out of control given the right circumstances.

Here's an example:

When I lived in Milwaukee, USA, it was often minus twenty-seven degrees Celsius during the winter. I had a three-month-old baby and a three-year-old toddler and my health had deteriorated to the point where I felt dizzy and about to pass out, every few minutes.

I was terrified of passing out in the car and either veering into the oncoming traffic, or fainting on the roadside and us all dying of hypothermia from the extreme conditions.

It seemed rational. I genuinely felt like I was about to pass out all the time, but it was irrational because (thankfully) I never actually did. The voice that said, 'You can drive the car, you'll be okay,' was quickly drowned out by the scream of my 'You're going to kill your children!' fear. Pretty soon, I was only driving when I absolutely needed to, and for short journeys. That was a helluva long winter.

This is what happens when our fear remains unchecked. Some people see this as a solution but pretty soon it turns into a coping strategy.

Popular coping strategies are alcohol, caffeine, drugs, sugar, exercise, violence, fatigue, and isolating ourselves. It's easy to see how any of these in excess can have a detrimental effect on our lives and the lives of those closest to us.

Thinking about Fear in a different way:

I have begun to see Fear as the friend who pushes me towards my purpose. It takes the sting out of the tail of fear and actually helps me to see the bigger picture.

Fear is always going to come up in your life and you need to make peace with it. Your goal is not to get rid of fear, but to re-frame it as the edge of your comfort zone, or as Author Mary Morrissey calls it, 'the border of the reality you know'.

Imagine getting an opportunity to fly to the moon. Excluding astronauts, most of us have never done travelled in space before and we know there's a fair element of risk involved so it would be very natural for us to have some fear around that. It doesn't mean we shouldn't fly to the moon. It just means we haven't done it so far. It's currently outside our comfort zone and so it brings up some fear for us.

Now try seeing fear as positive energy instead of a negative force. Imagine yourself at the 100m start line of the Olympics. You've trained and prepared and you're in good shape but as the starting gun is held aloft, you're aware of the adrenaline coursing through your veins. Isn't this just another form of fear? And in many ways couldn't that also be considered excitement? What if you could re-frame your fear in this positive way? What if you could focus on what you want to get out of the experience (your gold medal) rather than the fear that surrounds it? How would this allow you to take action?

You can try and outrun and outsmart fear but the fact is that it will always come up every time life offers you a challenge. Try to equate facing each fear with learning a lesson. The quicker you learn the lesson, the quicker it passes and the closer you are to becoming the person you are here to be.

The next time you feel the rush of fear, know it simply means you're about to step out of your comfort zone and don't let it hold you back. In fact, allow yourself little smile because you will get to know that outside of your comfort zone is where you'll have your most amazing life experiences.

Befriend your fear

Try making the fear welcome.

Get interested in what it's really about. Be willing to see things differently and you may just get an "ah-ha" moment. Many of your current fears are related to incidents that happened years ago and now seem completely irrational.

In my early thirties, I realised I was still carrying around a fear of abandonment that stemmed from my parent's divorce when I was five. This old fear had no place in my life but it was subconsciously affecting my beliefs and behaviour, despite the fact that I was a happily married woman with a loving family.

Once I witnessed and released this fear, I felt free to step into my own strength. I realised I could access what felt like a tidal wave of loving energy because I was no longer acting from a place of fear. Here's an exercise to help you:

Exercise: Befriend your fear

Write down the answers that come up for you. Don't censor or judge, just go with your first or instinctive answers.

My biggest fear is…

The earliest age I can remember having this fear is…

The message behind this fear is…

The effect this fear has on me is…

The truth about this fear is… (By this, I mean is this fear a real threat? Can you find evidence to the contrary anywhere in the world?)

I could re-frame this fear as…

I could be-friend this fear by…

The action I will take on this fear in the next 48hrs is…

Finish with 'I am willing to see things differently. I am willing to choose love and healing instead of fear.'

Block No 2 – Lack

Many years ago, when I was having a particularly bad health day, my husband offered to take me out to a lake near to where we lived. It was a beautiful autumn day in Wisconsin, USA and we were lucky enough to have the use of a lake cabin. There were so many reasons to go, but I was too stuck in my "I'm ill, I can't do it" mentality. I was caught up in my lack of health.

So I stayed home, alone. My husband took my kids and had a wonderful afternoon playing in the leaves up at the lake. Meanwhile, I sat at home, feeling miserable, wondering what the colours would be like and how the light would dapple through the trees. Sadly, I'll never know. That's an afternoon I'll never get back. What I do know is this. I'll never miss an opportunity again.

"Lack" is a trick of thinking that the ego plays on us and it can be very persuasive. If you hear yourself say or think "I'll never be", "I'll never have", or "I can't", then it's time to lose your lack perspective.

Here's how lack might show up and what you can do about it:

Belief – I'll never be healthy / I can't do that.

Action – Ask yourself, how can I see this differently? Look for small areas where you are abundant in life. Friends, family, someone who cares, a home, food on the table. These are all areas of abundance, right down to the flowers in your garden. Now look for small areas where you are abundant in health. Maybe you have pain somewhere but your vision is great. Maybe you have Irritable Bowel Syndrome but great hair. I could barely walk but I had great legs!

Appreciate what you do have and what you can do. Appreciate every improvement in your health however small. Stay in the present. The past is over and tomorrow you can start over, only this moment right now, matters.

Belief – I can't afford to eat healthily.

Action – Recognise that processed and unhealthy food is more costly than fruits and vegetables and the real cost is far greater in terms of your health insurance, hospital bills and medication, the cost of time off work or a job lost. Not to mention the cost of missing days, weeks, months, years of your life. Can you really put a price on missing the moments you could be spending with your loved ones?

Belief – I can't be healthy and keep doing my job/stay married/hold on to that relationship/live in this house/whatever.

Action – Look to yourself first to see if the answer is within. Often it's not the external circumstances that need to change, it's your thinking about the external circumstances and relating them to your health. Change your perception by deciding to see things differently. This means that you no longer need to react in the same way and can free yourself from the consequences of the thoughts, feelings or behaviour. It's a simple tool that immediately negates the power that is being used against you. You don't have to know what "differently" looks like, you just have to be open to something new. Release the hold your thinking has on your health and watch as circumstances transform.

Belief – I don't know how to be healthy/I can't do this.

Action – Get out of your confusion by taking action. The simple steps in this book are a great foundation from which to learn and grow. Health does not have to be a complicated or scientific puzzle. As Mary Morrissey taught me, 'Even the smallest steps, taken sequentially, will get you up Everest.'

Keep putting one foot in front of the other. Take one step towards health today and repeat tomorrow.

Belief – I don't know who I am without this condition.

Action – Take this great opportunity to find out. Get curious about why you're here. It's my experience that we are all here for a purpose. Wouldn't you like to discover yours? Re-visit the visualisation exercise and stretch it out until you get an idea of what you'd love to be doing with your life after you've rebuilt your health. Devote some time to personal reflection about how your experiences so far have shaped you and given you skills or qualities you may be able to use in the service of others, or the world. Turn inward for some quiet time and reflection and wait for answers and clues. You may be surprised at the information that drops in to inspire you.

Belief – It's not worth it.

Action – What this really means is "I'm not worth it". Don't let your lack of health become a lack of self-worth. This is where you are right now, not where you will be forever. Recognise that underneath the symptoms you are experiencing in your physical body is something much deeper. Whether or not you consider yourself spiritual, be open to the idea that the real you is untouched by physical illness. At your core, you are boundless energy which cannot be destroyed.

If that sounds a little "out there" remember this, when the sh*t hits the fan with our health, we all pray to something. We have an instinctive knowing that there's something bigger than us. Keep sight of this while you pass through the challenge of this phase of your health. You are learning. You are evolving. This is just what it looks like while you are rebuilding.

Belief – I'm not well enough to make changes.

Action – Denial is a common form of lack. We hold tight to our illness and say 'I can't because...' We proudly flaunt our labels and stay exactly where we are. I've done this MANY times, but each time I did, I effectively made a choice that kept me stuck, I felt what little energy I had contract even further. I walked away from many opportunities to help myself get better, only to kick myself later and ask, 'Why did I take so long to do this?'

Denial is believing you have to get something BEFORE you give, as though you need proof before you commit yourself, when all along the proof is within you. As the Dalai Lama said, 'Be the change you want to see.' In terms of your health, I loosely translate this as "Get on with it!"

Regardless of where you are in your health journey, there are numerous things you can start today, even from this book alone. Denial keeps you stuck. Taking action kicks it into touch. As a health practitioner, I've often heard people say, 'I haven't got time to do that.' To which I reply, 'Do you have time to be ill?' Everything is a choice.

Belief – Only the doctor can cure me.

Action – Stop giving your power away to an external source. If you're lucky, your doctor will be a valuable and open-minded source of support, but that does not make them a miracle worker. If you are in any way intimidated by your doctor or unable to voice your opinions on your treatment then it can be a recipe for disaster.

Any thought that you are not responsible for your own health only creates separation in you. Isolating your body from your mind and perpetuating fear. It is imperative that you own your symptoms, your illness, your history and your rebuild. Just as a person creates physical illness over time, so they can unravel it over time. Owning your illness is part of owning the cure.

Belief – I can't live without coffee / sugar / alcohol.

Action – Addictive beliefs and behaviour are detrimental to our health. The truth is that any human being can live on water and a bit of food. We are not dependent on any of the above substances but the chemical reaction they cause in our bodies causes us to think otherwise.

If you experience cravings for anything, cut it out. Get support if you need to but get rid of it from your life. Having it less, or having it less often is not a solution. If you are unwell then any substance that creates more stress for the body is a no-no.

It may not be easy. There may be a period of withdrawal. Turn to the "Techniques" discussed earlier in the book to support yourself through this. Re-balance your body with what it's really crying out for; in many cases this can be addressed nutritionally or with the help of supplements. Get help where you need it but make the mental commitment that addictive food or substances are not part of your rebuild.

Sugar was my biggest addiction. I was so exhausted all the time that I fooled myself into believing that it gave me energy. As someone suffering from severe hypoglycaemia, all it gave me was a rollercoaster ride of feeling awful. I eventually gave up sugar for two years and while the cravings took two weeks to subside, the mental clarity I experienced occurred within forty-eight hours. It was nothing short of amazing. You can do it.

Block No 3 – The Ego

'What is joyful to you is painful to the ego.' A Course in Miracles.

Or in other words, just when you think you're getting somewhere a little voice says, 'You can't have that…'

Here's the thing – If you continue to see your body as something separate from you then you will always be in a position of trying to control it. When you get a symptom you don't like do you ever attack your body? Do you say or think, "Why is it doing this to me?"

Sometimes, in defensive mode we often resort to tough love and slip into "I'll show you" (which is about as far from love and acceptance as we can get!). Understand this is really your ego talking and you'll be familiar with the voice, it's the one that sits on your shoulder and tells you that you're not good enough.

The ego's job is to compare you to other people. So if you see someone strong, healthy and pretty much as you'd like to be, and you slip into jealous and bitter thoughts about why your illness has happened to you. I can assure you that's your ego talking. By comparing you to others it makes you feel unworthy, unloved and unhealthy. From here, it's a hop skip and a jump into the victim mentality or "why is this happening to me?"

I really bought the "Ego" t-shirt on my illness. It had me hook, line and sinker and my response was to fight for control. Energy flows where attention goes, so whatever you think about you create more of. I was so focused on my poor health that I got more of, you guessed it, poor health.

My ego had a field day telling me I wasn't good enough. I'd let myself down and was basically a complete health failure. Not a good feeling. If you can relate, here's how to turn those feelings around and escape your ego.

Exercise: Escape your ego

Stop the separation

Rather than seeing your body as something external to yourself, or something you just happen to be wearing that day, begin to see yourself and your body as one. Your body responds to your mind but if the ego is running wild in your mind then it's not going to be pretty. Next time, the ego-driven thoughts of blame, shame, guilt, need or worth come up, try a little loving kindness.

Close your eyes, breathe deeply and change your perception to see yourself not as a mind and a body struggling for control, but as one. Connected and complete. Requiring nothing more in this moment that love and appreciation. By joining your perception, you are less likely to judge and compare, and more inclined to say, 'Wow, how did we get here and what can we do about it?'

Every time you hear the inner voice that chastises you for being unwell, blames the part of your body that's let you down, moans about your job, partner, or another circumstance for making you ill, take a deep breath and make a choice to let it go.

Repeat this phrase.

This thought does not heal me so I release it. I choose love instead.

I know when I started this practice, I was saying this about a hundred times a day. A lot of the time we're on autopilot, programming ourselves with negativity. If you want a stronger reminder then wear an elastic band around your wrist and every time you have a negative thought about your health, pull the band and then let it ping back against your skin. You'll experience a slight stinging sensation which should jolt you into remembering to let go.

When you transform your relationship with your body it may feel strange at first. Your ego may try and convince you that you must retain control and keep the separation, but I think you'll find it a relief to keep the drama of your health story at bay as you give yourself a chance to rebuild.

Re-connect with yourself and keep the ego separate. You'll be surprised at how your new thoughts of self-love and compassion guide you to new behaviours that support your health.

Here are some common perceptions from the ego:

I'm so unfit/ overweight / slow/ exhausted/ fat / ugly / sick/ worthless.

If you hear this internal voice or recurring thoughts telling you you'll never be well and perpetuating distrust of your own body. Then here's what you need to remind yourself, out loud!

> *Fear and judgement cannot exist in the presence of love so I perceive myself through loving eyes. I'm recovering from… and I need to rest a little more. I can accept I am working through an illness. I welcome the opportunity to change that this situation brings.*

The ego fosters resentment as it always wants something. Whereas seeing your body lovingly as a connected part of your whole, brings love, compassion and forgiveness which reduces the stress and anxiety you experience.

Can you feel the difference? Can you remind yourself of the statement above when you hear your ego kick in? Repeat it to yourself as often as required.

How can I be sure if it's my ego talking?

The simple rule here is: if it feels like restriction or constriction, it's the ego.

When the ego speaks to us, it often has a sense of judgement attached to it, or a need to prove something.

If you have a great idea or inspiration around something that would help your healing and then immediately a negative thought pops in, that's the ego.

Block No 4 – Forgiveness

If you really want to be well then you need to make peace with your past and your present. Period. You need to be happy in yourself and in your life regardless of what's happened and what's to come.

Holding resentment is one of the most common blocks that prevent good health showing up in your life. To make peace with your past forgiveness must happen. You have to let it go and if you're about to put the book down now and say, 'She just doesn't get it.' I do. Read on.

Whatever has happened to get you to this point is OVER. I have said this before but it's worth repeating. Shame, blame and judgement create ill health so make a conscious choice to give them up, now.

Even the wrong choices can take us to the right places.

Everything that's happened has brought you to this point. All that matters is the present and you're here for a reason. This is the right place from which you begin the rest of your day and the rest of your life.

> *The power of forgiveness is that you do it FOR yourself and you do not need to forgive the behaviour just the being.*

So if someone tortured, abused you or murdered a loved one then of course you cannot forgive that behaviour, but you can try to forgive an unskilled human being, who knew no better than to act out of a lower emotion than love.

When people act out of fear, anger, ignorance, hatred, jealousy or resentment, recognise that really they're acting out of pain and a lack of love in their own lives. It's doesn't condone their behaviour but it helps you to understand that it's their stuff only you can choose if it's going to keep affecting YOU!

This is a practice. It does not happen overnight, but is possible.

If you don't believe me, or you're finding it impossible to forgive someone, please go to the resources page of the rebuild website and listen to and watch the Forgiveness audios and videos.

Why is Forgiving essential to my rebuild?

You don't forgive FOR the other person. You forgive FOR yourself. You forgive FOR the freedom it creates in you, because you no longer have to carry around the pain, hurt and grief. This means you have space for something else – namely, love and healing.

Forgiveness doesn't change the past but it changes the present and it changes your future. It creates a shift in your perception to help you see things differently. It removes the block in you.

Recognise your potential in THIS moment. Forgive FOR your health.

If you find this idea difficult, go deeper, it's probably a reflection of something you don't like about yourself. None of us wants to admit this but the sooner we do the sooner we can release it. You don't need to announce it to anyone else, there's no need to take out a 1-page ad in the local paper damning yourself. Just decide to forgive yourself too.

Forgive yourself for being unwell or below par. Forgive yourself for any guilt, blame, shame or unskilful behaviour you may have exhibited as part of your illness. Make amends where you can and move on.

Remember, forgiveness is giving FOR yourself and it's a process, not a one-time event. Make it a daily practice until you begin to feel some release.

Make peace with your body and your illness

We have all seen a mother nestling a hurt child to her breast. We may have even done this ourselves or experienced it as an outpouring of love from our own mothers. Now's the time to find that love within and direct it towards the place that is unwell. This is far more powerful than you can imagine if done with true meaning and forgiveness.

Block No 5 – Gratitude

Now that you are feeling more peaceful and connected, it's a good time to talk about Gratitude. Without an appreciation for the good that we have in our lives, however small it may seem, it's very hard to attract more of it. By taking a daily dose of vitamin G, you'll learn to appreciate what you do have and create more of it in a lasting and fulfilling way.

When you wake each morning, spend a few minutes going through all the things that you are grateful for. Make a quick list and reflect upon it during the day, if you feel yourself dropping into negativity or despondency.

Repeat the exercise at night, finding new things to add. No matter how small. You can be grateful for just being here, being alive on this day and having the chance to change.

Why gratitude is essential?

'As I give so I shall receive.'

If you're focussed on fear and ill health, that's what you're "giving out" and so guess what you get back? Exactly the same. Without gratitude for the good in your life you close yourself down to receiving more good. Take love as an example:

The truth is that the more love we let in, the more love we are able to give and the more we give, the more open we are to receiving. There is no limit to love.

If you're denying someone love, or projecting anger at them, then anger and a lack of love are what you'll receive in return.

In the book *A Course in Miracles*, the text explains that you will only experience lack in the areas where you are not giving. So if you want to attract more love into your life, be more loving to everyone and everything. If you want more health, give out the frequency of health. This means eating well, resting, looking after yourself, and reading positive and uplifting material.

The more you open yourself up to great health, the more you are willing to receive support that helps you to create great health, the more health will flow to you. If you are really stagnated in any area then be grateful for what you do have and find a way to give.

Simple ways to give:

- *Volunteer*

- *Chat to someone on a park bench or the bus*

- *Do something nice for someone*

- *Donate to charity*

- *Mentor someone*

If you are someone who battles with negativity, make this an ongoing practice and you will be amazed at how good you feel just from being of service and helping others.

> *If you want to help yourself, help someone else.*

If you want health, create an intention for someone else's health. If prayer works for you, pray for their health, recovery, or rebuild. Take out all judgement and notice what happens to your vibration when you make this a practice for thirty days. You don't have to know this person, it might actually be better if you don't, as then you won't be tempted to project any beliefs about their chances of survival or the way their recovery should happen. Instead, hold an open-minded intention that they will make a full recovery and notice what happens to the way YOU feel as a result.

Being able to receive

Maybe you're not comfortable receiving?

If you're ill and feeling a lot of blame, shame or guilt around your condition then it may feel impossible for you to receive help, support or love, because you're judging yourself or feel you don't deserve it. Let's do a quick check of how you're receiving.

- *Think about the last time someone paid you a compliment. Did you smile and accept it graciously or brush it off?*

- *When people offer you help or support. How do you receive it?*

Gladly?

Willingly?

Gratefully?

Or do you brush it off?

Do you refuse it?

Deny you need it or feel ashamed by it?

For the next month could you be more open to receiving?

Could you make this a conscious practice?

Here's what you need to know:

As the great Sufi poet, Rumi, said:

> *'What you seek is seeking you.'*

We, not our circumstances, are the creators of health. Great health doesn't happen in the future, it happens now. It starts now with your thoughts and beliefs and actions. Great health is always available for you.

In essence, all we're really giving and allowing ourselves to receive is love, in some form or another. Just think about that for a second. Every act of giving you make, at a deeper level is an act of love. You may see it as kindness, generosity, gratitude, charity, or something else but it all comes from a place of love. Make a practice of giving and receiving with grace, gratitude and appreciation.

To listen to a guided Gratitude exercise, go the resources page of the rebuild website.

Block No 6 – Taking Action

At some point in your health journey, you're going to get to a fork in the road.

You can read this book, put it on the shelf and never look at it again. You can earmark pages and pretend you'll come back to them or you can close it entirely. You can tell yourself you'll do it later, when you have "time".

What you can't do now though is pretend you don't know this stuff. If you're not ready or willing to take responsibility for your own health, that's also your choice. I hope it brings the results you want because the truth is, the only person with ultimate control over whether or not you'll be well again, is you.

In his brilliant book *Emergence, Seven Steps for Radical Life Change*, author Derek Rydall says:

> *'Action is belief in work clothes.'*

He's right. Anything less than action is denial and denial only keeps you stuck. If you buy into denial – and your ego will come up with all kinds of crazy reasons why you should – then trust me, in a few years you'll find this book, read through it and think, why the hell didn't I do this?

When you take action, do it from the right frame of mind. Never act out of fear, anger, hate, denial, jealousy, greed or malice. When you take action from any of these negative states you will notice a kind of friction, and an internal sense that just doesn't feel good. A gut instinct that this isn't the best choice. The result will NEVER lead you to a healthier state. If you act out of love, kindness, or a desire for something greater you are far more likely to benefit.

Take action, or visualise taking action now, as if you are already healthy. You may not be able to get out of bed but wiggle your toes, stretch your arms and legs, breathe! Think and take action as though you are the vibrant, energised person in the vision you created earlier in the book.

You MUST become a vibrational match for health and vitality.

When I was ill, I had information I didn't use, all around me. I read countless books and put them back on the shelf ready for when "I felt better". I wasted a lot of time procrastinating and the absolute truth is that it was my choice.

What will you choose?

How to take action

1. Look back at the worksheets you've completed in this book. Reflect on your journey so far and see this point as a fork in the road. Here you can make the choice to move in the direction of wellness, or you can continue on your current path. Decide to be responsible for your health.

2. Notice where you feel conflicted and take action in these areas first. Taking the bull by the horns will give you a sense of empowerment that change is in your hands.

3. Chunk it. Have you ever heard the question, 'How do you eat an elephant?' Answer, 'One bite at a time.' The elephant is your rebuild so don't try to do it all in one bite. Break it into do-able chunks and build up from there.

4. Strip away your false beliefs and write some new ones. Remember it's an inside job. Neither the source of your illness or the solution to it, are outside of you. From this point forward, you are a work in progress. Change the way you see the problem and eventually the problem will cease to exist.

5. Set goals and have a coach or mentor hold you accountable in a supportive and positive way

6. Allocate "Healing" time every day and develop a practice that works for you. Whether it's quiet time for reflection or a gentle walk outside where you appreciate everything around you. Be patient. Just as it takes time to create imbalance in our bodies, so it takes time to unravel.

7. Read and mentally and emotionally step into your health vision daily. Find within it an inner reason to live. The more you can engage with the feeling tone of it, the faster it will become a reality. Act from the point of great health, even if you don't feel it yet. It will push you to try new things, be they diet, exercise or purely information.

8. Come from a mindset of health, not illness. Focus on the opportunity to be well not the current problem of illness. Don't let your current perception of what you can't do, get in the way of what you can do to create health.

Block No 7 – Support

The more supported you feel, the faster you will achieve your health goals. Don't try and rely on your willpower. If that was going to be enough, you wouldn't be here now. You don't need to do this alone. Just as a shared intention is stronger, so a supported rebuild is stronger and more successful.

I guarantee you will meet many people along the way, some of whom may change your life forever. I am eternally grateful for the gifted and talented people who have helped and enlightened me on my journey.

A good place to start is the Rebuild Your Health community. Join us and discover that, that as you support others, you are in fact healing yourself at the same time.

There is an old saying, 'The giver of the rose bears the scent.' This means that to help and support someone else you have to energetically put yourself into a healing space and your body feels the benefits of this at a cellular level.

The Rebuild community believes in seeing your potential for health, rather than your current state of health.

How NOT to use support?

There were definitely times when I found myself relying on others when a health crisis flared up. When you find someone who understands you and your symptoms it's tempting to give them all your power, and make them responsible for healing you.

Some days, I would call a particular practitioner and beg her to see me. If she couldn't, I would quickly sink into the misery of not believing I was responsible for my health. Secretly, I think she knew this and was helping me to stand on my own two feet. She knew I was strong enough and, in time, I learnt to borrow a little of her belief in me.

When you "have" to see a particular practitioner to stop you going to pieces, you know the ego is in control and you have handed over responsibility.

Your greatest power is always within.

This is the time to remember that only you can heal yourself. You may need medical support or an operation, but what you believe about your ability to heal ultimately determines the outcome. The minute you hand that responsibility over to someone else, you diminish your ability to ever be fully well. You are much stronger than you know ☺

Getting to the Gift

Many people I meet who have suffered with illness only ever talk of their experience in terms of its negative aspects. They're still holding onto the pain of it, rather than the learning.

Remember the saying, 'Every cloud has a silver lining.' I am a great believer that bad health isn't all bad news. In fact, ill health can be a gift, albeit in unusual wrapping. In Bernie Siegel's book, *Love, Medicine and Miracles*, many cancer sufferers came to see their condition as a gift. A wake-up call that led to huge changes in their lives.

The gift of my health crisis was a wake-up call that led to radical changes in my life which have propelled me into a far more rewarding career. It gave me an opportunity to re-think my life and make different choices.

What's the gift of your illness?

It may sound crazy but entertain the idea that there's a greater purpose at play here. As you work through the exercise below I hope you'll find some silver linings of your own.

Exercise: Getting to the gift

What behaviour have you changed as a result of your health issues?

Why do you think you had to experience this illness? What has it forced you to do or learn?

How is this illness serving you? What is illness allowing you to do, or not do?

How has illness changed your relationships?

Which relationships have begun or ended as a result of this relationship?

Who have you met and which new friends do you have as a result of your illness?

Is being ill the only way you can get support or be listened to?

Does your condition allow someone else to care for you in a particular way or give you attention?

How has illness affected or changed your job or profession?

What have you been forced to stop doing and what are you doing instead?

Who would you have to be and what might you have to do, if you were healthy and strong?

Why does this create fear for you?

What life changes for the better have you undertaken?

Can you see what the gift, or learning, in your illness is?

Is there something you're resisting?

Surrendering to the gift

Whatever you fight you fuel. What you resist persists.

If you're caught in the drama of your condition, if you're stuck in your perception of your circumstances, then now's the time to surrender to the gift and move on.

Research your condition, disease or illness thoroughly enough and you will find someone who has overcome it. Use their story as a model for how to take the power out of the problem. They declared their illness impotent and wrote a new story of health for themselves. They made a choice. You can too.

Illness may not seem like the nicest gift to open, but if you approach ill health with humility and curiosity you will get to know yourself better than ever before. This is the blessing of what initially looks like a curse.

Illness is the entry ticket to your journey of self-actualisation. Welcome the opportunity to learn as you are re-directed towards health. Believe something better lies ahead and understand that we do not heal in one moment, but rather at one moment after another. Look for the gift ☺

Head in the direction of health and hold your course. You will reach your destination.

Journal Space

SECTION 9

YOUR 8-STEP ONGOING PROGRAMME

Follow these eight simple steps to stay on track throughout your rebuild.

1. Learn how to listen

Sometimes we don't listen until it becomes really inconvenient, or until it becomes life-threatening. Symptoms are your body's way of communicating with you. There is always a message. Remember to listen.

2. Develop a passion for your own potential

Stay in the mindset of possibility. Remain alive to your potential. It's not about the destination it's about the journey. It's who you become in the process. It's the calm and the peace that you feel inside and how connected you know feel to yourself and others. It's how empowered you feel to lead your life and make changes to support yourself.

Reframe your health crisis and turn it into a strength that you can draw from. Don't give power to the symptom, disease or condition. Illness is just an opportunity to heal. Change your thinking about it and watch your circumstances change.

3. Trust there's an answer to every question

There's a solution to your health crisis. You just don't know it yet! Don't defer it to someone else – ladies, don't defer to a man! Work through this process. Trust it. When you feel insecure you defer power to others. Take it back now. Change your perception of healing, make it welcome, grow into the new you. You can embrace your ability to heal.

4. Accept your past

Everything happens for a reason and sometimes the wrong choices bring us to the right places. Forgive FOR yourself. Forgive FOR your health.

5. Become your own best friend

'I've finally stopped running away from myself. Who else is there better to be?' Goldie Hawn.

Can you see your body is your best friend?

If your best friend was standing in front of you now – would you ignore, berate, or criticise them? If they were saying, 'I'm malnourished, I'm struggling,' would you throw them a packet of crisps and promise to be healthy next week?

Start treating your body as your best friend. Be grateful for everything it does to keep you alive and above all, be loving.

6. Own your story

I have shared my story with you. My hope is that the journey it resulted in, and the learning it required, has helped you, in some way, on your health journey. If you doubt your potential to be well, look to my example and that of countless others and recognise that what is possible for one is possible for all.

7. Consider a spiritual practice

Suffering and sickness come from a feeling of separation. If you can find a practice that works for you, be it meditation, a new thought movement, or yoga, you will feel the separation ease. The realisation that you are not alone can give you the courage and strength you need. Faith in something greater than yourself is powerful. Prayer works for countless people. Be willing to explore your own spirituality.

It is NOT about religion. If religion works for you as a concept then move in that direction. If it doesn't, look for a group of positive thinking, likeminded people who can hold you in your healthiest potential.

8. Start today

I'm going to encourage you to try this out for 40 days. Actually, I'm encouraging you to try this for life, but 40 days is a good start. I love action because it results in change. It keeps us open to possibility and gets us back in the flow of life.

Now is the time for a revolution in health. I invite you to become part of a generation of Rebuilders, ready to take responsibility for their health and well equipped to do so. Measure your success in terms of how happy, peaceful and balanced you feel, and the physical wellness you seek will happen.

Embrace this journey. Accept healing as your birthright. Transform your relationship with yourself and your health and reclaim the life you know is possible.

Your health is a choice. Choose well.

Finally...

So it's well over a decade since I started my rebuild. Who am I now?

I'm the woman I thought I'd lost forever. Actually, I'm a far better version of her, and if I can do it, it means you can too. Knowing how to make yourself happy and healthy is such a relief. It finally means you can stop waiting for someone else to do it for you. It means you can take back control.

Use this book. Re-do the exercises and worksheets periodically to demonstrate your progress. Join the rebuild community and become part of a movement for better education around health and empowerment around health choices. Use your experience to help others. Be a guiding light for someone in need. Be a beacon of love for yourself.

It's time to rebuild. It's time to reclaim. It's time to live.

SECTION 10

RESOURCES

Here you will find the tools I used in my rebuild and continue to use to help me stay on course. I hope they are as helpful to you as they are to me. Use them as a springboard to your own vitality.

Where to get more info on sugar

There's more info on why you should avoid sugar than I have space for in this book.

If you want more info in an easily accessible format, try watching *Simply Raw: Reversing Diabetes in 30 Days*, an independent documentary film that chronicles six Americans with "incurable" diabetes switching their diet and getting off insulin.

Doing a RAW diet may not be viable for you but 10-20% RAW is a possibility for most of us and if nothing else, it will prove to you that the body can heal, if given the right conditions and support.

I also highly recommend Dr Mark Hyman's book *The 10-Day Detox Diet* which has excellent, easily accessible information on why to avoid and how to manage sugar in our diets.

Books I loved!

- *Love, Medicine and Miracles* – Bernie Siegel, M.D.

- *Food: Your Miracle Medicine* – Jean Carper.

- *Eat Right for Your Type* – Dr Peter J. D'Adamo.

- *The Age of Miracles* – Marianne Williamson.

- *Nourishing Traditions* – Sally Fallon.

- *Emergence Seven Steps for Radical Life Change* – Derek Rydall.

- *The Blood Sugar Solution 10-Day Detox Diet* – Dr Mark Hyman.

- *You Can Heal Your Life* – Louise L. Hay.

- *Cellular Awakening* – Barbara Wren.

- *From Fatigued to Fantastic* – Jacob Teitelbaum, M.D.

- *A Cancer Therapy* – Max Gerson, M.D.

- *Staying Healthy with Nutrition* – Elson M.Haas, M.D.

- *Prescription for Nutritional Healing* – Phyllis A.Balch and James F.Balch, M.D.

- *Low Blood Sugar* – Martin L.Budd.

- *The Oil Protein Diet* – Dr Johanna Budwig.

- *The Biology of Belief* – Bruce H.Lipton, Ph.D.

- *Philosophy of Natural Therapeutics* – Dr Henry Lindlahr.

- *The Oil That Heals* – William A. McGarey, M.D.

Alternative therapies I used and loved:

Homeopathy – by far this made the biggest difference in my rebuild. Simply astounding results.

Cranio-sacral – a great practitioner will release emotional and physical stress.

Reflexology – a lovely relaxing and de-stressing treatment that can support particular organs.

Chinese Herbs, Acupuncture and Moxibustion – To open up energy meridians and release blockages.

Bio-Resonance treatments – Using electromagnetic waves to diagnose and treat illness.

Reiki – A relaxing, releasing and healing experience.

Acupuncture and Moxibustion – Using needles and heat to clear blocked energy meridians.

Journey Therapy (based on the book by Brandon Bays) – A deep, soul searching experience to facilitate healing of past traumas.

NIA – A combination of dance, yoga and martial arts – for me it was a joyful releasing and strengthening process.

Emotional Freedom Technique (EFT or Tapping)

There are many alternative therapies available today – see what you are naturally attracted to and use them as support rather than a cure. I worked through several, over a period of years as I needed them. No one therapy cured me, but they helped me release and heal so that I could heal myself.